Angie Molkentin

Wanting to Give God Your Whole Heart

NORTHWESTERN PUBLISHING HOUSE
Milwaukee, Wisconsin

Cover Photo: Shutterstock
Art Director: Karen Knutson
Cover Concept and Series Logo: Matthew Bown
Designer: Paula Clemons

Northwestern Publishing House
1250 N. 113th St., Milwaukee, WI 53226-3284
www.nph.net
© 2018 Northwestern Publishing House
Published 2018
Printed in the United States of America
ISBN 978-0-8100-2933-0
ISBN 978-0-8100-2934-7 (e-book)

18 19 20 21 22 23 24 25 26 27   10   9   8   7   6   5   4   3   2   1

Contents

"It sort of dawned on me that love was the answer. . . .
It seems like the underlying theme to the universe."

—*John Lennon*

Prologue

On a sunny summer day, I happened to take a road trip with Carrie. Our teenage sons were headed to a Christian summer camp to be counselors for a week. I was grateful for Carrie's company. She's a wonderful Christian mother, very selfless and wise. I could learn a lot from Carrie during a three-hour drive.

We talked about our kids, balancing busy schedules, church work, and other blessings of our very full lives. We talked about things we love to do—Carrie is a wonderful musician—and how busy moms can find time to enjoy things they love to do while also serving those around them. I can't speak for Carrie; however, I enjoyed the conversation so immensely that at one point I turned the wrong way out of a rest stop and drove in the wrong direction for a few miles before realizing my error. We had a laugh as I turned the car around. Good company creates a bad sense of direction, I guess.

A few weeks later, I received a call from Carrie's husband, an editor for Northwestern Publishing House, who asked if I'd be willing to take part in an experiment. (Carrie had suggested me to him.) The experiment was to revolve around the topic of "loving God more." The assignment, in a nutshell, was to spend 180 days studying a topic, praying about it, observing those around me, and recording the experience in a journal. Several others were taking part in the project, studying their own topics for 180 days. Project participants would then use their experiences to write a book on their topic. The project had what seemed to me to be a clever name: "My 180."

I was taken aback by the invitation to do this. As a writer in the public relations field, my specialty is writing for other people. I'm essentially a ghost writer. I listen to other people, learn their voice, learn what they want to say, and put words to paper under their byline. I am invisible. So to write something about my own experiences, with my own byline, would be unnerving.

And then there's the topic: love. Let me assure you, nothing in particular qualifies me to teach anyone about love. Yet the more I prayed and considered this project, the more I wondered if God was calling me to study love precisely because he knew I needed to study love. I'm not one of those people who walks around exuding God's love (although I appreciate people who do). And I'm not one to be particularly considerate of others. I'm more likely to greet my husband with a honey-do list than a hug. Yet I know God created me with emotions. I've been known to throw a pretty good temper tantrum. And I've been known to get caught up in emotional thinking, causing me to take a wrong turn now and then. So studying the greatest of all emotions—love—seemed as though it might be beneficial.

Could I fit the work into my busy life? Well, I'd have to prioritize. After all, isn't that what God commands us to do where love for him is concerned? "Love the LORD your God with all your heart and with all your soul and with all your strength" (Deuteronomy 6:5). Maybe I would learn something from this project, and other busy people could benefit from what I learn.

And so I said yes. I forged ahead on this journey, equipped with prayer, the Word, and an accountability partner riding shotgun. This book chronicles how my 180 journey was helpful for learning about myself and chronicles what God showed me through others along the way. Though written in the first person, it's not really a book about me. It's about God working through me, using "My 180" as the vehicle.

You may wish to try a "180" yourself. No matter where you are in your faith life, I believe you can benefit from a 180 journey. You may have a little knowledge of the Bible or a lot, faith that can move mountains or faith the size of a mustard seed. A 180 journey is not about where you begin or even where you end. It's about the journey itself, the God who guides it, and the people you meet or observe along the way. I invite you to take note of what you see as you journey with me, perhaps in preparation to make a 180 journey of your own. (I've included "Travel Tips" specifically for those who wish to embark on their own journey.) If you're simply a backseat rider on my journey, I've included reflection opportunities to help you make the most of our time together.

I pray that God uses my humble story to bless all those who wish to make a similar journey.

A Love Story

"Bring back that lovin' feelin'."

— The Righteous Brothers

My husband and I are raising three children, all teenagers at the moment. Our life is busy and a bit chaotic. The simple routines we tried to establish for our household when the kids were younger have fallen away in favor of keeping up with each family member's schedule and commitments. Jon and I tag-team to keep everything going smoothly. As a result, there is little time for Jon and me to spend together as a couple. Try as we might, the relationship we had before kids has taken a backseat to the blessings and busyness of raising kids.

We often joke about what life will be like when the children leave the house. We will spend more time together because there will be no one to interrupt, no games to watch, no school activities to manage. We'll have to rediscover why we liked each other in the first place. We're anticipating that new phase in life, excited for the time to reacquaint after years of relationship autopilot.

It's possible for a relationship with God to be put on autopilot too. I consider myself a devout Christian, and yet I often find myself putting off or hurrying through my Bible study or prayer because "more important things" are in front of me. I know God will always be there, and I have every intention to spend time with him once I get through this busy day, week, month. It's a dangerous slippery slope.

God wants a loving relationship with his people. He even longs for it. He describes what he is looking for through the prophet Jeremiah: "I remember the devotion of your youth, how as a bride you loved me and followed me through the wilderness, through a land not sown" (Jeremiah 2:2). Jeremiah was called to speak these words to the people of Israel, to call them to repentance and back to a loving relationship with God. It was meant to be a beautiful relationship—with both reverence and feeling—like newlyweds who profess their love and feel the excitement of a new beginning. They have committed their lives to each other, excited to explore whatever terrain stretches before them with a faithful companion at their side.

This book is about rediscovering, rekindling, guarding, and keeping that kind of love in the life of a Christian. As the chapters unfold, they reveal the gradual progression I made through the power of the Holy Spirit toward a better understanding of God's love for me and my love for him. God communicated with me through his Word and sacraments. (We'll talk more about those in a bit.) I communicated with him by reading his Word and through prayer. In response to my prayers, and because he knows my needs, God sent specific people into my life at various times to illuminate certain truths about loving him. The stories of those individuals, and what I learned from them, are peppered throughout these chapters.

As you and I journey through these chapters together, I hope you'll see, as I did, that God is the author and perfecter of our faith. He guides the journeys of his people, even as we follow him into lands not yet sown.

Survey the Landscape

Let's say you're planning a trip to Disneyland. Given the size-able investment of this trip, you'd likely assemble a file of "all things Disney." You would read reviews and learn everything you can from others who've been there. You'd probably look up the weather patterns for the time of year you intend to travel, so you know how to pack. You would research the best modes of transportation. All this would serve to prepare you and to fuel your excitement for the trip.

I began my 180 journey with a little research to understand the topic I was about to study. Before I committed to a study plan, I simply Googled "love" and related topics. I wasn't exactly sure what I was looking for, and it wasn't an exhaustive research project. I simply thought that doing a little research might provide a good list of topics to journal about during my 180 journey.

I Googled things like "most famous love song," "famous love poems," "how many times does the word *love* appear in the Bible?" and "famous quotes about love."

The exercise was kind of fun, and it sparked my creativity. I didn't know exactly how I would use the information—I just thought it might be nice to know what had already been written about the topic of love.

It. Was. A. Lot. Check out the next chapter and you'll see what I mean.

I could let the volume of material and the broad topic intimidate me, or I could forge ahead and figure out how I (and my relationship with God) fit into the chorus of voices and myriad of opinions about love. I decided to forge ahead. As I did so, I felt the same nervous energy I feel on the day I leave for a big vacation.

I reassured myself: *I'm not an expert on love, but it's a great topic. Many have studied it before me. I've assembled enough facts and opinions to know that this is going to be a great trip. It's time to get going.*

TRAVEL TIPS:

If you are considering a 180 journey of your own:

- ○ **Think about some topics you might want to explore** during a 180 journey. You, like me, might choose "loving God more" as your topic. There are other worthy topics as well, such as "trusting God more" or "praying to God more."
- ○ **Be curious** about your topic!
- ○ **Assemble a little research** to inspire your study plan. I used internet searches, books from my own bookshelf, and observations of people and situations that crossed my path or came to mind as I was preparing for my study.

This Thing Called Love

"But the greatest of these is love."

In 1967, the Beatles were asked to write a song for the Our World Project, which was to be broadcast in 24 countries across five continents. They chose to write a song with a simple message of love and peace that could be understood by all the varied people tuning in across the globe. "All You Need Is Love" made its debut to the largest television audience ever up to that date, an estimated 400 to 700 million people. The word *love* is sung 111 times in the anthem. Google it to read the lyrics or give it a listen.

The Beatles understood something about love—it is perhaps one of the most unifying elements of the human experience. It can be seen, felt, and heard all around us: The look in someone's eyes. The reassuring touch of a hand. The whisper of the most significant three words in the English language, *I love you*. Throughout time, love has been written about, sung about, and studied intently in an effort to understand it or to commend its power to influence human conditions and actions. "Love is energy of life," Robert Browning wrote. The word *love* appears 2,191 times in the works of Shakespeare, who is often credited with creating some of the most insightful literature on the subject. And during one of the most tumultuous times in our nation's history, Martin Luther King Jr. said, "Love is the only force capable of transforming an enemy into a friend."

Technically speaking, *love* is both a noun and a verb. We can both love someone (an action) or be in love with someone (a state of being). People are commended for their acts of love even when the feeling of love isn't there, and the feeling of being in love has been described as the most glorious, most consuming, and most valuable of all emotions: "the star to every wandering bark [sailing ship]," Shakespeare wrote. Ironically, many people in pursuit of the feeling of love as a noun abandon the action of love as a verb.

As I surveyed the landscape, I narrowed my examination of love in the broad human experience to a Christian perspective. Even then, the topic was still enormous. Here are a few broad observations about love and Christianity:

Love is the central theme of Christianity. Christians believe that the Bible is essentially a generations-long love story between God and the people he chose to be his own. The Bible's books and chapters all serve to chronicle the promises God made to his people and the ultimate demonstration of his love through his own Son, Jesus Christ. Through the fulfillment of his promises, God reveals himself as a God who loves all people.

- God declared his everlasting love for his people through the Bible's Old Testament prophets such as Hosea, Jeremiah, and Isaiah.

- Love for all people was the compelling reason for Jesus' birth, life, death, and resurrection as revealed to us in the iconic John 3:16—one of the most well-known verses in the Bible (which, incidentally, is often displayed by zealous Christians via tattoos, banners on highway overpasses, and signs in the crowd at major league ballparks): *"God so loved the world that he gave his one and only Son, that whoever believes in him shall not perish but have eternal life."*

- The command "love one another" or "love each other" appears at least 15 times in the Bible, all in the New Testament (New International Version, 2011). It is especially prevalent in the book of John, including John 13:34; 13:35; 15:12; and 15:17.

- The Bible repeatedly says that there is nothing God wants more from us than our love. The "greatest commandment" is first given in Deuteronomy 6:5: "Love the LORD your God with all your heart and with all your soul and with all your strength." That passage is repeated twice in the New Testament— in Matthew 22:35-40 and in Mark 12:28-34.

Love is an attribute of God, as described at length in 1 John 4, and it has its own list of attributes, as described in 1 Corinthians 13. Paul declares love to be the greatest of all Christian attributes in 1 Corinthians 13:13 and the motivating factor behind all Christian actions in 2 Corinthians 5:14.

Love is the top-ranked search topic on Bible Gateway, the world's most popular app for accessing the Bible. The word *love* is used 551 times in the New International Version of the Bible (2011)—319 times in the Old Testament and 232 times in the New Testament. The Bible wasn't written in English, yet because the word *love* is used so often on its pages, many novice Bible scholars like me have learned various Greek words for the word *love*. For example, I've been told that the Greek word *phileo* means love in the sense of being friendly—the kind of love that forms from senses and emotion. Then there's the Greek word *agapao,* the form used by the writers of the Bible for more deeply spiritual matters. The *Encyclopedia of the Bible* says that *agapao* is "love founded on admiration, veneration, and esteem. It means to have a preference for, wish well to, regard the welfare of. It is to be full of good will both in thought and deed."

It's about now that my head begins to hurt. As I survey the landscape on the topic of love, I realize that I've only scratched the surface in terms of understanding its significance in our world. What about the meaning of the word *love* in other languages? for other cultures? for people who lived at other points in history? for me personally?

No matter how I look at it, love's impact on the world is astounding. People have done amazing and radical things in the name of love. In the case of Christians, Christ's love for us has compelled ordinary people to become martyrs, missionaries, crusaders (yikes!), emancipators, reformers, nurses, philanthropists, and friends to the friendless. Love is the status, the compelling reason, and the unlimited power source behind everything *truly* Christian that has happened and is happening in this world. For those who aren't necessarily Christian, the idea of love still has power. In fact, it was the unifying power of this simple, four-letter word that the Beatles sought to tap in the summer of 1967 when they wrote "All You Need Is Love."

Given the enduring presence and role of love in our world, learning more about it seems like a wise endeavor. I'll keep forging ahead.

As I do, there is one niggling thought I can't get out of my head—that passage from Deuteronomy that is called the greatest commandment: *"Love the LORD your God with all your heart and with all your soul and with all your strength."*

God commands us to love him. What does that mean? Why is it called the greatest commandment? Who are some good role models for loving God? How can I learn from them and love God more?

↻ ①. ↺

WHY LOVE GOD MORE?

Head and Heart

"Start with why."

—Simon Sinek

I did not realize how little I understood God's love for me, or the meaning of love, until I went through my 180 journey.

It all started with a simple question: *Why?*

Why love God more? What is the motivation to do so? If I could first put my finger on the motivation, I would be able to turn up the love, like a dial. And that would be a good thing, right?

I work in the public relations (PR) profession, which means I basically smooth out relationships for a living. In business, there are usually things that can be done to enhance a relationship, deepen it, and make it mutually beneficial. My job is to search for those strategies and help clients act on those strategies. Usually, the PR plan starts with a simple analysis:

- Who is the audience?
- What do we want the audience to know, think, or do differently?
- Why? What is in it for the audience? How do we create buy-in to manage change?
- What are we going to do to achieve the desired outcome?

That's a strategic PR plan in a nutshell. It's used for everything from selling widgets to electing candidates to changing public opinion on social issues. In the course of my career, I have tackled many issues and helped many clients through distressing situations. With a good plan, many target audiences can go from a place of little-to-no information to a place of greater understanding or from uninspired to inspired.

1

With this project, logically, I saw myself as a target audience that needed to be moved to a better place. When I examined my situation, I found that the *head knowledge* was all there from my years of catechism class. (See sidebar "Here's What I Know.") To create change, head knowledge needed to be paired with a *favorable attitude* toward loving God more. To assess my own attitude, I wrote down the questions that swirled around in my head:

- Does it really matter if I love God more?

- Will God notice if I love him more?

- Will my life look different if I love God more?

- I think I love God. Why don't I *feel* it?

- Does my level of enthusiasm matter to God?

- Even if I lived with great enthusiasm, would it really matter to those around me? God's will is going to be done with me or without me.

I must admit . . . I felt guilty for asking these questions. They revealed a less-than-favorable attitude toward changing my behavior. How could a person who was raised by Christian parents, sent to Christian schools (at great financial sacrifice on the part of my parents), and an active member in her church be so lukewarm in her attitude about loving God? I knew that I could not expect results for this journey without confronting my attitude. No PR plan is successful unless the target audience develops a favorable attitude toward change. My attitude was indifferent at best— and maybe much worse, as you'll read a few short chapters later.

Okay. Let's assume that I *do* want to love God more. (Why would I invest myself in a 180 journey if I *didn't* want to love him more?) What would success look like? I wrote down some thoughts:

- I want to move from being a Christian with head knowledge about God to being a Christian with a willing heart to act on that knowledge.

- I want to be a person who exudes the love of Christ, so others can see it and give glory to God.

- I want to actually *feel* love for God.

As I prepped for my 180 journey, some of my Christian head knowledge resurfaced and helped me realize that I was not alone in my quest to live a more passionate Christian life. Others have been on this quest before me, and perhaps I could learn something from them. For example,

I've always loved reading stories about Martin Luther and other Christians who lived in and around the time of the Reformation, that period of great change and awakening in the Christian church that took place five hundred years ago. I'm fascinated by the passion and courage these Christians displayed and by the way the world was transformed not only religiously, but also economically, culturally, and politically during this time period. I recalled reading a book a number of years ago—in fact, it's still on my bookshelf—that described how a group of reformers attempted to give Christian living a shot in the arm. I pulled the book off my shelf and jotted down some notes about Philipp Jakob Spener, a German pastor living in Frankfurt almost a century following the Reformation.

At that time, Spener was growing increasingly worried that Lutheran Christians were becoming lukewarm, unfeeling, and consequently less spiritual. Not content with lukewarm, Spener organized his congregation into small groups devoted to prayer and Bible study. The motivation behind Spener's revival work, in his own words, was:

> . . . to establish among Christian individuals a holy and close friendship, that each one learns to recognize the Christianity of the others whereby the fire of love is more and more inflamed among us, from which so much passionate desire arises that everyone may be edified at every opportunity and by their example may excite others next to them to heartfelt earnestness. (*Dreyzehn Theologische Sendschreiben,* 1716, quoted in *Sanctification: Christ in Action* by Harold Senkbeil, page 28.)

"Fire of love" and "passionate desire." These are the feelings I was missing at the beginning of my 180 journey. Spener's prescription was studying the Bible and following the example of other such "inflamed" Christians. Granted, many Bible-believing theologians in Spener's time asserted that he went too far, that he and theologians like him placed undue emphasis on our feelings toward God and not enough emphasis on *what God has objectively done for us*, irrespective of our feelings. Many knowledgeable Christians today also agree that Spener went too far. Nevertheless, the reformer was confronting what he believed to be the absence of "heartfelt earnestness," and there is nothing inherently wrong with asking ourselves whether that type of zeal is missing from our Christian living. The apostle Paul writes in the book of Romans, "Never be lacking in zeal, but keep your spiritual fervor, serving the Lord" (12:11).

And later in 2 Corinthians Paul says, "Examine yourselves to see whether you are in the faith" (13:5).

My 180 journey would certainly be a vehicle for examining myself—probably more than I ever have in my entire life as a Christian. I was hopeful that the process would ignite what I wanted to feel: "zeal" and "heartfelt earnestness" beyond head knowledge. After all, what God wants is clear: *"Love the LORD your God with all your heart and with all your soul and with all your strength."*

Clearly it's not enough to *know* with my head alone. God wants all of me: heart, soul, strength. I know this command in my head. I want my heart to follow suit. How does that happen?

YOUR TURN:

- What do you know to be true about God? About his relationship with you?
- How would you describe your attitude toward God?
- What is your answer to the question, Why love God more?
- What do you think "loving God more" would look like in your life?

Here's What I Know

If you are new to Christianity or if you have not opened your Bible or catechism in a while (or don't even know what a catechism is), you may benefit from me taking a little time to share what I know to be true about my relationship with God. I call it *head knowledge* because, by God's grace, the information is all there in my head, thanks to my Christian parents, pastors, and teachers.

You may not start your journey in exactly the same place mine started, and that does not matter. I simply want you to understand where I began.

First and foremost, I believe that the Bible is God's Word and presents objective truths about God and his relationship with me. I've listed the truths and the Bible references here so that you can review them for yourself.

○ God created the world, and when he did so, everything was perfect. (Genesis 1)

○ The first human beings, Adam and Eve, were real people who rebelled against God. When they did, they were no longer perfect. Sin and death entered the world and have since been passed along through the generations to every human being. (Genesis 3)

○ Now sin, like a deep chasm, separates humans from one another and from God. He made us to be loving people who rely on him and rejoice in him. Instead, from birth we are self-absorbed, proud people who could hardly care less about God or others. (Isaiah 59:2; Romans 3:23)

○ I am in this same predicament. From birth, my every heart's desire has been inclined toward evil, and this separates me from God. Even when I feel like I'm not so bad, that inclination is there. (Genesis 8:21; Psalm 51:5)

○ I, like all human beings, need something or someone to make me right with God again. I can't do it myself, no matter how hard I try to be good. (Romans 3:19-24)

○ God loves all human beings, and so he came up with a plan: He sent Jesus to make things right between God and all human beings, including me. Jesus did that by taking on the punishment for all the world's wrongdoing in our place. (Psalm 145:9; Luke 19:10; Isaiah 53:5)

○ Instead of asking me to earn, even in part, my way into his love and acceptance, God says, *Simply believe that Jesus has already earned it for you.* (Acts 16:30,31)

○ I know that God was not obliged to tell me the good news about Jesus. He has told me only because of his grace, his overflowing generosity. (1 Peter 2:9; 2 Thessalonians 2:16)

○ I know that it is only because of his grace, his generous heart, that God keeps me in the faith, keeps me believing in what Jesus has done. (1 Peter 1:5)

○ I know that, out of love and thankfulness to my Savior, I will serve God and bring glory to him with my actions. (Colossians 3:17)

○ God wants me to share what I know with others. (Matthew 28:18-20; Luke 8:39)

TRAVEL TIPS:

As you consider your own 180 journey:

○ **Evaluate your starting point:** What is your relationship with God like right now? What do you *know* to be true about your relationship with God? How do your *actions* reflect what you know? Are there any gaps between what you *know* and how you *act?*

○ **Establish your goals:** What might you want to accomplish during a 180 journey? What improvements would you hope to see in your relationship with God?

5

Why 180?

"We should handle it the best way we know how and get on with it. That's what my mind says, I just wish somebody would explain it to my heart."

—M'lynn Eatenton, *Steel Magnolias*

As I prepared for my 180 journey, I was really in tune with anything that fed into what I intended to study. Love songs, love quotes in movies, Bible stories about love—I perked up and listened more intently to all these things. So when I sat in on a Bible study about Esther, I couldn't help but notice the opening chapter and its relationship to my study topic.

The opening lines of the book of Esther describe a banquet given by King Xerxes, the powerful ruler of the Persian Empire from about 486 to 465 B.C. Anybody who was anyone in Persia at the time was present at this banquet. All the nobles and military leaders came to feast, revel, and undoubtedly dream about their next great conquests. The palace was decked to the nines. Food was plentiful and drinks were flowing. Important leaders in the government mingled, and prominent citizens from the four corners of the land came to pay their respects. King Xerxes was using the occasion to make a statement. "For a full 180 days he displayed the vast wealth of his kingdom and the splendor and glory of his majesty" (Esther 1:4).

A 180-day party! Six months of eating and drinking and reveling! Bible-believing historians surmise that King Xerxes intended this banquet to be the kickoff for an immense military campaign—an unsurpassed display of his wealth and power that would build unwavering loyalty to him. Small rebellions had started to break out across the empire, and Xerxes likely wanted to convey that he held the same wealth and power as his father, Darius I. Xerxes and his advisors must have deemed that 180 days was a sufficient amount of time to display such power. (As it turned out, God had plans of his own. The 180-day revelry set God's plans in motion for Esther to become queen and to play a prominent role in preserving and protecting the Jewish people.)

One hundred eighty days seems like a ridiculous amount of time to party. Likewise, in today's society, it seems like a ridiculous amount of time for a Bible study on one topic. In fact, I'm quite sure that a book with the title *180 Days to a New You* would sit on the shelf and gather dust. The human attention span averages eight seconds. Or 140 characters if you tweet. We only have time for one click or at the very most "three easy steps." Even the famed 12-step process seems so yesterday. One-minute devotions pop up on our phone apps, and Christian radio in the car keeps us on the straight and narrow even if the day does not allow for 15 minutes alone with God.

Not that there is anything wrong with trying to fit Bible study into the hustle and bustle of a busy life. In fact, the Bible encourages it: "These are the commands. . . . Talk about them . . . when you walk along the road" (Deuteronomy 6:1,7). "Pray continually" (1 Thessalonians 5:17). And professionals often deliver Bible studies and devotions right to my mobile phone, free of charge! What a blessing it is to have God's Word curated, organized, and sent to us in bite-sized servings to grab-and-go all day long.

The prospect of a 180-day project made it abundantly clear how overreliant I was on these modern tools. I had been fitting God into my life instead of putting God first, yielding to his leadership, and building my life around him. And now I was holding this invitation in my hand: *"Love the LORD your God with all your heart and with all your soul and with all your strength."*

What if I spent 180 days studying this concept of putting God first? Feasting on God's words. Drinking in his Holy Spirit through the Word. Marveling at the beauty around me and the people who come in and out of my circle at various times. Would I experience all the beauty and joy and peace that loving God more has to offer?

I believe God wanted me to rediscover the story of Esther—this little gem in Scripture about a 180-day party designed to ward off rebellion. King Xerxes may have sensed that dissidents were lurking, waiting for the opportunity to weaken his kingdom from the inside. Likewise, I sensed that I needed to take intentional and deliberate steps to confront the rebellion that was brewing in me.

YOUR TURN:

- Have you ever taken on a self-improvement project of any kind? What was it? How long were you committed to the project?

- Do you think you could study the topic of "loving God more" for a full 180 days?

- What might stand in your way?

- What personal weaknesses might you address with a 180 journey of your own?

Rebellion

"The spirit is willing, but the flesh is weak."
—Matthew 26:41

I met Rebellion very early on in my 180 journey. I have to hand it to her: She was one of the most persistent of all the friends and acquaintances I observed during this project. She had a habit of dropping in unexpectedly and drawing me into conversations that I really didn't have time to have.

Once in a while, I entertained her. After all, she did bring up some seemingly valid points from time to time. She made me think.

One evening I was reading from the book of Deuteronomy in the Bible's Old Testament. In this section of Scripture, God is speaking through Moses to the Israelites before they finally enter the land God had promised to them generations previously: *"Be careful that you do not forget the LORD, who brought you out of Egypt, out of the land of slavery"* (6:12).

As I read, I recalled my *head knowledge* about this part of Israelite history: how God had saved them from a very desperate situation. They had been cruelly, even murderously, enslaved by the Egyptians. God then raised up a leader among them, Moses, to defy the Egyptian pharaoh and lead the Israelites out of Egypt toward their freedom (the grand "exit" for which the book of Exodus is named—depicted with critical acclaim in the movie *The Ten Commandments,* with Charlton Heston as Moses).

I recalled what I am supposed to see in these verses: first, how God protected his people, and second, the parallel to my own life. God rescued both the Israelites and me from desperate situations. He rescued the Israelites from a life sentence of making mud bricks under the hot Egyptian sun. He rescued me from the sin that separates me from God, a death sentence for my soul. (The apostle Paul called us "slaves to sin" in Romans 6:6.) Deuteronomy is a historical narrative about the people of Israel; it is also a reminder for all God's children to revere him and to be thankful for his deliverance. Like the people of Israel, I ought to remember the Lord who brought me out of my predicament.

This is when Rebellion brought her first challenge. She invited herself into my home, stood beside me as I studied, and began asking questions.

"If somebody saves you from a desperate situation and says, 'Now you have to love me,' is that real love?"

"It is," I replied. "If God had not rescued me, I would remain forever separated from him."

That's what I learned in catechism class. That's what the Bible says.

"Seriously? God commands people to love him?" Rebellion queried innocently.

"He loved me first," I answered, recalling the memory passage from 1 John 4:19. "So I love him back."

"Seems a bit condescending on God's part," Rebellion observed. "He threatens to abandon you, he swoops in to save you, and then he commands you to love him."

I looked up from my Bible, exasperated. I glanced around at the untidy room, the dishes still undone in the kitchen, the clock with its small arm pointing to the 10. I didn't have time for Rebellion's questions. I simply wanted to finish my study, get my housework done, and get to bed.

Rebellion followed my gaze and quickly picked up on my frustration. She surveyed the clutter and then looked at me with one raised eyebrow. In this pose, she reminded me of the Dowager Countess of *Downton Abbey*, trying to appear magnanimous and all the while judging me for today's unfinished work.

I met her unspoken judgment head-on. "None of this matters," I said, gesturing to the piles of paperwork and dinner dishes on the kitchen counter. "God loves me and he saved me and that is what is important here. Please let me finish my study."

"By all means, continue," Rebellion insisted. She pushed aside some clutter and sat down beside me. A few minutes passed.

"Are you thankful that he saved you?" she probed.

I was annoyed. I was just trying to get my devotion and my housework done before 11 P.M., and she wanted to have a deep theological conversation?

She persisted. "Well? Are you thankful?"

I had to think about that a bit. The fact that I had to think about it pricked my conscience. I knew I should be thankful. Truth was, I did not *feel* very thankful at the moment, and she knew it.

"Oh, I don't know!" I finally said, incensed. "What does it matter? I know I'm saved; I thank God whenever I think of it, end of story."

"So you must feel special that you are one of 'God's children,'" she continued. She made air quotes with her bony fingers for emphasis.

My mind was filled with a million things to say to her, but as debates went, she had me on the ropes. She was making an emotional appeal and I was armed with facts. I threw a few of the most critical facts her way, including what I knew to be true from my catechism study: Jesus "purchased and won me from all sins, from death, and from the power of the devil, not with gold or silver but with his holy, precious blood and with his innocent suffering and death. All this he did that I should be his own, and live under him in his kingdom, and serve him in everlasting righteousness, innocence, and blessedness" (Explanation of the Second Article of the Apostles' Creed, Luther's Catechism, 1998).

"Why would God do such a thing? Why would he bother with you? So you can serve him?" Rebellion's eyebrow arched again.

"Yes. It's a privilege to serve him."

"Sounds fun," Rebellion retorted.

"Yes, it is!" I exclaimed. I'm sure I did not sound convincing. I felt compelled to add, "I delight greatly in the LORD; my soul rejoices in my God. For he has clothed me with garments of salvation and arrayed me in a robe of his righteousness" (Isaiah 61:10).

"You have a funny way of looking 'delightful.'" She made air quotes again.

After I concluded my devotion, she sat for quite a while and watched me finish up my housework. She must have known I wanted her to leave by the way I was slamming cupboard doors and muttering under my breath. But she didn't leave. Finally, when I announced I was calling it a day, she stood up and surveyed my work.

"None of this matters," she whispered in my ear, tossing my earlier words right back at me.

I gestured toward the door. Then I saw my journal sitting on the table next to my Bible. I opened it and wrote, *"Day 1 of My 180. Does God really command me to love him? Do I owe him love for rescuing me? Why does that make me bristle? Lord, help me confront this."*

I glanced up from the page, and Rebellion was gone.

She visited me often during my 180 journey. It should have been easy to slap her assaults down with head knowledge and not let her get a word in edgewise. I was supposed to "put on the full armor of God" and "extinguish all the flaming arrows of the evil one" who sent her to me (Ephesians 6:11,16). But she said some things that touched a nerve: Am I thankful? Do I feel grateful?

The command rang in my ear: *Love the Lord your God with all your heart, soul, strength.*

God wants all of me. It is not enough to love with the mind but not with the heart and soul. The Bible's language in that command means "with all your being." If I love with head knowledge only, I am depriving God of what he asks for. What he *commands.*

YOUR TURN:

- When it comes to loving God, does Rebellion ever visit you?
- What buttons does Rebellion push for you?
- What do you know about God's love for you that you can use to steel yourself against Rebellion's way of thinking?
- What are some ways you can confront Rebellion's challenges? Might a journal work for you?

You Don't Need to Know *Why* to Start

If you're thinking about doing a 180 journey in an effort to explore "loving God more" (or any topic, really), be assured that you don't have to have all the answers when you start. That's why you're doing the journey!

I did not know the answer to "why love God more?" when I started. What I did know, however, is that I wanted to live a more passionate and emotive Christian life. I wanted to *feel* more love for God and for others around me. And, as David wished in Psalm 51, I wanted to feel the joy of my salvation.

The beauty of a 180 journey is God's Word combined with prayer and an emotional outlet—a journal. These are your primary tools. God's Word is the objective truth that balances the subjective and volatile human emotions explored on the pages of the journal. The journal becomes an important tool for self-reflection over time. And prayer is your way of channeling all your emotions toward God, who will use them for his purposes.

TRAVEL TIPS:

- ○ **Find a good study Bible.** I used the *Concordia Self-Study Bible,* New International Version, that my husband and I received as a wedding gift.

- ○ **Purchase or set up a journal**—either pen and paper or electronic. I used old-fashioned pen and paper because I use a computer a lot during the day and I wanted my 180 time to feel different.

- ○ **Put your tools in a place where you will see them every day** and be reminded of your commitment.

(II.)

CAN I LOVE GOD MORE?

What I Did

"We are not yet what we shall be, but we are growing toward it, the process is not yet finished, but it is going on, this is not the end, but it is the road."
—Martin Luther in *Defense of All the Articles*

In the early days of my 180 journey, I craved the feelings of peace and joy that I assumed would accompany loving God more, yet the only emotions I felt were more the negative sort. Rebellion visited often, and I felt guilty for entertaining her. I didn't have time for the fights she tried to pick. Early on, it seemed easier and more godly to set emotion aside than to deal with Rebellion's questions. Lukewarm was comfortable.

And it was getting me nowhere.

So I used my journal to turn up the heat, and that became a place for me to safely explore Rebellion's questions. I allowed myself the luxury of a written temper tantrum every time I thought about loving God more. I'm not proud of the words and thoughts in those first few weeks of my journal: They reveal everything from apathy to confusion to outright rebellion against God for asking me to do more than I was already doing or felt capable of doing. I know from raising kids that temper tantrums are driven by emotions and usually take place when something is out of balance. Typically, emotions are brought back into balance with calm and discipline.

What could be more disciplined than a 180-day Bible study? What started out as a healthy challenge turned out to be the perfect way to confront a brewing rebellion. My 180 was a process that included these elements:

1. Praying every day for . . .

    a. help to love God more,

    b. help to understand better what it means to love God more, and

    c. help to notice other people around me who are good examples of loving God more.

2. Studying every week the Bible's teachings about loving God.

3. Talking every week with my friend and accountability partner who agreed to go on the same journey.

4. Journaling each day about what I was learning and experiencing.

I created a study plan with a slightly different focus each week, so as to explore the many aspects of loving God more. The study plan included Scripture, as well as a few readings from notable authors on the subject of loving God. (See sidebar "How Did I Know What to Study?")

The experiment was designed to explore whether a disciplined period of time in the Word and prayer on a particular topic would help me understand that topic better and, in turn, produce changes in my life. To help me with my discipline, I created a calendar to check off the days. (As a busy mom, checklists always work well for me.) I kept the calendar tucked in my journal.

I set myself up so there would be no excuses. Much like a couch-to-5K runner sets alarms on his app or a person with weight-loss goals keeps an inspirational photo on her refrigerator door, I kept my 180 materials in the hub of my home so they were part of my daily routine. For the next 180 days, my Bible study and journaling were to be as much a part of my daily life as eating and picking up after the kids.

I did not allow multitasking. That is, I did not allow myself to do my 180 work while I was driving the kids, watching TV, cooking dinner, etc. No reading and journaling while in the waiting room at the dentist office. It had to be dedicated time, whether it was 15 minutes or 45 minutes.

If you are already a disciplined student of God's Word, and devotion and prayer are part of your daily routine, I commend you. Your approach to a 180 project might bring different benefits. You already have the discipline and you may benefit from the in-depth study of a particular topic. I have to believe, however, that out there are many busy people like me whose prayer and devotion life could benefit from a 180 in ways never imagined. There is incredible blessing in being devoted to a task for a long period of time. The art of long-term devotion is lost on so many of us in our modern society. And multitasking has become a high art.

There were days when I did not have a quiet moment to myself until late in the evening. (Okay, many days!) My journal contains many pages where I lamented, *"It's 11 P.M. and I am just sitting down to do my devotion and journal now. I'm tired. Where did this day go?"* This caused me to question where my priorities were and how I might be able to rearrange them to put God first. Had I allowed myself to multitask, I never would have questioned my priorities. I probably would have thought of myself as pretty organized, adept at juggling everything in my daily schedule.

There were also days when I was bored with the topic of loving God. *"Some of the Bible references this week seem repetitive, and I don't feel like there is anything new being revealed to me this week"* (journal entry from Day 63). This too had its purpose. Noting that I was bored usually had one of two results: I augmented my study to read something new that piqued my interest, or I acknowledged that devotion to God was difficult and I needed his help. Each result had its benefits.

And then there were the people. Each day I prayed to notice people who were good examples of loving God. It amazed me how God brought people into my life at just the right time to punctuate an idea or illustrate a concept from his Word. I wrote about them in my journal, but I never told any of them I was doing so—at least not until after my 180 journey was complete. I wanted the interactions to be natural. I wanted to "be still" (Psalm 46:10) and let God bring the examples to light.

Oh, what a feeling

I began this chapter describing the role Rebellion played in my 180 journey. While I am not proud of the thoughts and attitudes she exposed in my heart, the questions she asked were key to getting this party started. I believe a private journal, when combined with the study of God's Word, provides a safe place to explore human emotion and to ask God to use emotion for good. The physical discipline required to do a 180 project, coupled with the emotions poured out on the pages of my journal, helped me see how God uses both the spiritual and the physical, the emotional and the logical, to keep us close to him. As long as we live in our mortal bodies, we will experience a tug-of-war between these aspects of ourselves. God intends to bless us through the struggle.

And herein lies one of the greatest learnings from my 180 journey: In the pages of my journal, I find that my emotions and the objective facts about my relationship with God are often at odds with one another, and it is only when the Word works on my heart that these two are brought together into a powerful confidence that produces feelings of gratitude and joy. The Holy Spirit working through the Word has the power to harness my emotions and use them for God's glory. That is his intent. That is the joyous state Mary was in when she sang, "My soul glorifies the Lord and my spirit rejoices in God my Savior" (Luke 1:47). Or that David was in when he wrote, "Praise the LORD, my soul; all my inmost being, praise his holy name" (Psalm 103:1). Or that Peter was in when he spontaneously jumped into the water, clothes and all, to see Jesus (John 21:7).

Oh, to live with such feeling! Oh, to exude such joy and confidence every day! What a full life that would be! And that is exactly what God wants for us. Not only does he want all *of* us—heart, soul, mind—he also wants all *for* us—all the good things that make life full and invigorating. "I have come that they may have life, and have it to the full" (John 10:10). He created us as emotional beings, both spirit and flesh, and he is Lord over all of it. He displayed his power over both these parts of the human condition many times:

- He did it for the disciples on the road to Emmaus, whose downcast faces reflected their weary spirits little more than 24 hours after they had witnessed the abuse and crucifixion of Jesus (Luke 24:13-35). Jesus cleared up their confusion by the end of their evening together.

- He did it for Mary and Martha, who, in their frustration, challenged him: "'Lord,' Martha said to Jesus, 'if you had been here, my brother would not have died'" (John 11:21). Jesus resolved their frustration by raising Lazarus to life that same day.

- He did it for Jacob, who (while apprehensively awaiting the arrival of his old enemy and brother Esau with four hundred armed men) wrestled with God and declared, "I will not let you go unless you bless me" (Genesis 32:26). The next day Jacob's reunion with Esau was peaceful.

- He did it for Peter, who was so astonished at Jesus' power that, when he first met Jesus, he emotionally exclaimed, "Go away from me, Lord; I am a sinful man!" (Luke 5:8). Instead of going away, Jesus invited Peter into his inner circle of friends.

- He did it for Job, who, in his distress, cried out at God, "Why have you made me your target?" (Job 7:20). After many trials (and many chapters in the book of Job), "the LORD blessed the latter part of Job's life more than the former part" (Job 42:12).

In each of the above situations, we see God's people struggling with human emotions. I included the references for each story so you can go back and dig into each one. (See sidebar "Brushing Up on Bible Basics" for more suggestions.) You'll notice how in some of the stories, the characters were well-equipped with head knowledge of who God is and the power he has. Still, when confronted with real-life tragedies or with surprises that had their minds reeling, their human emotions bubbled up and over. In other cases, the characters were missing key pieces of factual information, and they really didn't know what God was planning to do. Emotions filled the void. In *every* case, God was present during these emotional struggles. For this reason, it is imperative that anyone who embarks on a 180 journey keeps God's Word close at hand. Rebellion is a dangerous guest, and conversing with her without God's presence in his Word brings disastrous consequences.

Witness the biblical character Cain, who faced a struggle between what he knew in his head and what he felt in his heart. Cain seemed to have higher regard for his prize fruits and vegetables than he had for God. Meanwhile, his brother Abel brought big portions of his wealth to God in tribute. We aren't told in the Bible precisely what Cain and Abel were thinking about their offerings; we are told that "the LORD looked with favor on Abel and his offering" (Genesis 4:4), and not so with Cain's. This frustrated Cain, and he grew jealous of Abel. God confronted Cain, warning him: "Sin is crouching at your door, . . . but you must rule over it" (Genesis 4:7). What did God mean by this? Sinful emotions were threatening to take over Cain's heart. Cain had to stop them, control them, change them. Cain didn't. He could've handed all of his emotions over to God; instead, he handed himself over to his emotion. He committed the world's first murder. Then he walked away from God—unrepentant, unyielding, and forever lonely.

When I think about that story, I seriously ask myself, what if I am Cain? Not that I'm worried I'm about to murder someone . . . but what if Rebellion continues to knock and I let her in and, one day, she decides to take up residence in my heart? I repeat the prayer that was mine every day of my 180 journey: *O Lord, please be the God of my heart, soul, and mind. Renew my strength and be present whenever Rebellion visits. Help me to love you more. Help me to better understand what it means to love you. And help me to notice and learn from other people who are good examples of loving you.*

YOUR TURN:

- Think of a time when you felt extreme emotion toward God. What were those emotions? Gratitude? Peace? Joy? Sorrow over sin? Frustration? Weariness?

- Think particularly about the negative emotions: What happens when you allow these emotions to consume you?

- Now think about the positive emotions: Do you see them as a blessing? Would you like to experience these emotions more?

- What tools can you use to regulate the negative and inspire the positive?

How Did I Know What to Study?

The Appendix contains a study guide I used for my 180 journey. I began with the "greatest commandment" for reasons described in a later chapter, and then, by using my study Bible's concordance, I chose portions of Scripture to study and tried to organize them in a somewhat logical fashion. (A concordance lets you find all the verses in the Bible that have a certain word in them: for example, all the verses that have "love" or "loving" in them. Some Bibles contain a concordance. You could also use the search function on a website like biblegateway.com for this.)

Each week of my study had a general theme. Early on I focused on passages that highlight God's love toward humankind, then I focused on passages that describe what love and loving God look like. I listed a different passage for each day of my study and chose one passage to be the focus of my study with my accountability partner each week.

I also assembled a few excerpts from books and Christian writings on the topic of "loving God" that I thought would be helpful. I built in two weeks of "flexible" study time, just in case I ran across a passage that needed more attention. This flex time was really helpful, because there were indeed times when I needed to review key concepts or dig deeper into an idea.

I'm sure that a pastor would have come up with a much more organized study than I did. My goal was not to create the perfect Bible study plan. I simply wanted to start reading what the Bible says about love and—through 180 days of prayer, journaling, and daily experiences—let the connections fall into place. Through it all, I remembered what God promises with regard to his Word: "It will not return to me empty, but will accomplish what I desire and achieve the purpose for which I sent it" (Isaiah 55:11).

If you decide to try a 180 journey of your own, I suggest a similar process for creating your study:

○ Do a little internet research, and spend a little time in your study Bible's concordance.

○ Assemble a few chapters or excerpts from books and Christian writings related to the journey you have chosen.

○ Organize it all in some logical or topical fashion.

○ Then let the process—and God's Spirit—do the work.

Brushing Up on Bible Basics

You've undoubtedly noticed that I'm weaving Bible characters and passages into this story about my 180 journey. That's because during my journey, something amazing happened: The Holy Spirit jogged my memory and dusted off those stories that lay dormant in the far corners of my mind. Characters sprang to life and new connections were made. The stories I learned as a child took on new meaning as I studied them with a new context.

I'd love for you to have this experience too. If it's been a while since you read the Bible, you might enjoy picking up a child's Bible history book—you know, one of those easy reads with beautiful pictures. Most church libraries have a plethora of these books on hand. One I like is *The Story Bible: 130 Stories of God's Love* (ESV).

TRAVEL TIPS:

○ **Consider reading a Bible story a day** from a children's Bible history book as part of your 180 journey.

○ **Ask yourself what each story teaches you** about God's love for you or your love for God.

○ **Pray** that God will bless your reading, increase your understanding of what it means to love God more, and show you real-life examples of people who love God.

○ **Enjoy** how God makes connections for you!

Sarah

*"She speaks with wisdom, and
faithful instruction is on her tongue."*
—Proverbs 31:26

I knew that success for this project would depend on a strong, wise accountability partner. I have many wonderful Christian friends, but there was clearly one choice: Sarah.

Sarah is incredibly steady. I've known her since college, where she was active in the campus ministry. She knew my husband before I did. During those college days, whether rollicking or stressful, Sarah always appeared to be a steady and faithful Christian woman.

Throughout the years after graduation, I received letters from Sarah, always handwritten. And this was at a time when computers were starting to make it very easy to print typewritten letters with address labels. Nearly every year a Christmas letter (again, handwritten) would arrive that told what Sarah's growing family had done throughout the year and that proclaimed the joyous news of Christ's birth.

I remember the year her letter told about her mom's illness. Then her husband's stroke. Then her mother's death. I remember the sadness in her writing. Still, she wrote. My bulletin board would be filled with "Happy Holidays" postcards, and Sarah's greetings would come folded, 2-3 pages, tucked in an envelope, faithfully telling of the year's events and giving God the glory.

God brought Sarah into my life again when we both moved to the same area and our daughters had the opportunity to attend high school together. We saw each other more frequently around school, sat in the bleachers together at games, and visited after concerts. To my mind, Sarah had not changed much. She was still the incredibly wise, steady Christian woman who clearly loved God.

What a perfect accountability partner.

I must confess, another reason I asked Sarah to be my accountability partner is I knew she would be able to make the time. We're all blessed with the same amount of time each day, yet most modern women would say they never have enough. Sarah would say that too. She has been a stay-at-home mom faithfully for 20 years. She is often asked to volunteer, head committees, or step in when someone needs assistance. I've noticed that Sarah chooses carefully so that she does not overextend herself with volunteer activities.

When Sarah talks about her life, she acknowledges that she is blessed to be able to stay at home. In the past, she often wondered if she should be jumping back into the workforce. She determined that her work was in the home and in being a strong Christian woman for those who need her. And, I might add, *available.* So many of us fill up our schedules so that when someone needs a kind word, a ride, a meal, or an accountability partner, there is not a minute to spare. We pass by on the other side of the road, en route to somewhere "more important."

Sarah has ordered her life in such a way that she is available to serve. That is her way of loving God. She was the first person I thought of when I needed someone I could observe who would meet with me regularly, who would hold me accountable.

Sarah and I met weekly to discuss our study and our journaling. My emotions during this project bounced up and down, back and forth. Sarah remained steady. There was a calm about her that most people might attribute to genes, although my visits with her revealed more than that. Sarah is in God's Word in a disciplined way every day. She applies God's Word in her life. My 180 was not a heavy lift for her.

And so Sarah became the first person I observed "loving God" during my 180. I don't think I fully appreciated Sarah until I reached the end of my 180 and reviewed all the examples I had observed of people loving God. All the qualities I noted in people . . . Sarah has them all.

YOUR TURN:

- Who might you choose as an accountability partner for a 180 journey of your own?
- What godly qualities does that person have that could be a blessing to you on your journey?

How to Hold Yourself Accountable

If you embark on a 180 journey, you'll quickly find that 180 days is a long time! At the end of any given day, you might be staring at "11:00" on your clock, wondering if you have either the energy to do your study or the ideas to write in a journal. That's where an accountability partner comes in.

Sarah and I met in person weekly—almost every Friday morning—to discuss our week of studies and what we had recorded in our journals. Sarah had a copy of the study plan and followed along, although the more important aspect of her job was to make sure *I* stuck with the program. She listened to me as I shared my discoveries and encouraged me when I felt stuck.

Does your accountability partner have to be a Christian? Well, we know from the Bible that having a Christian friend is extremely valuable. Solomon wrote in Ecclesiastes: "Two are better than one, because they have a good return for their labor: If either of them falls down, one can help the other up. . . . Though one may be overpowered, two can defend themselves. A cord of three strands is not quickly broken" (4:9,10,12).

You already know from my story thus far that a 180 journey requires balance between objective biblical truths and emotions. When emotions overpower, a Christian accountability partner can use God's Word to help restore balance. And you can pray together. I have been taught that the "cord of three strands" Solomon talks about includes two friends *and their God.*

Your accountability partner can study alongside you or simply check in with you periodically. I found it helpful to meet at regular intervals (weekly) and in person. The meetings also could be accomplished via Skype, FaceTime, or telephone. The methods and quantity of meetings are not as important as the type of person you choose.

Here are some qualities of a good accountability partner:

○ **Devoted to God's Word as the source of truth.** This is vitally important because your emotions may carry you off track. You need someone who will bring you back to the center—God's Word.

○ **Available to you for the next six months.** Choose someone who will have the time to check in with you or periodically meet with you. If you feel you are burdening this person with your requests to meet, you're less likely to meet, and there goes your accountability.

○ **A good listener.** You want your accountability partner to listen to your reactions to your readings and to listen to what you write in your journal. He or she can then ask probing and clarifying questions.

○ **Trustworthy.** What happens in your journal stays between you and your accountability partner.

○ **Wields a velvet hammer.** If you fall off in your commitment, your accountability partner is not afraid to call you on the carpet. He or she can be gentle but firm.

○ **Will pray with you and for you.** Prayer is a very big part of a 180 journey. It is the method for channeling all those emotions away from your own heart—where they could simmer and stew and maybe mislead—toward God, who can "renew a steadfast spirit" (Psalm 51:10) and even use your emotion for good.

What God Wants

"God comes, takes hold of the heart, and says: Learn to know Me. —Why, who are you? —I am Christ; I have plunged into your wretchedness, have drowned your sin in My righteousness. —This knowledge softens your heart."
—Martin Luther, *What Luther Says*, #2564

Now that you know how my 180 journey came to be and what I actually did to get on the road, I'll begin the process of sharing a little more about what I gradually learned as the days and weeks progressed. It's amazing to look back now and see how God was guiding my journey. In the beginning I didn't feel very confident that this would be a worthwhile journey, and I was especially uncomfortable confronting Rebellion's questions. I had to put a little trust in my study plan and my process and let things unfold.

Knowing that the goal of my 180 journey was "loving God more," as I have said before, it seemed logical to start by studying the "greatest commandment," as it is called: "Love the LORD your God with all your heart and with all your soul and with all your strength." It is first given in Deuteronomy chapter 6 and then (according to my self-study Bible) repeated in Matthew and Mark, where Jesus says that the entire Bible hinges on this commandment.

Let's take a look:

> Hear, O Israel: The LORD our God, the LORD is one. Love the LORD your God with all your heart and with all your soul and with all your strength. (Deuteronomy 6:4,5)

> Jesus replied: "'Love the Lord your God with all your heart and with all your soul and with all your mind.' This is the first and greatest commandment. And the second is like it: 'Love your neighbor as yourself.' All the Law and the Prophets hang on these two commandments." (Matthew 22:37-40)

> One of the teachers of the law came and heard them debating. Noticing that Jesus had given them a good answer, he asked him, "Of all the commandments,

which is the most important?" "The most important one," answered Jesus, "is this: 'Hear O Israel: The Lord our God, the Lord is one. Love the Lord your God with all your heart and with all your soul and with all your mind and with all your strength.' The second is this: 'Love your neighbor as yourself.' There is no commandment greater than these." (Mark 12:28-31)

In her earlier visit, Rebellion had suggested that a truly loving God would not command love. *Merriam-Webster* defines *love* as "strong affection for another arising out of kinship or personal ties." Or, as a verb, "to feel affection." How can God command someone to feel? Is that what this command is about?

As I asked myself these questions, my head knowledge reminded me that God can command us to love him because he is God and we are his creatures. He can do whatever he pleases. There is no greater reminder of this than in Job chapters 38–41, where God gives the emotional and questioning Job a stern reminder of his wisdom and authority: "Who is this that obscures my plans with words without knowledge? Brace yourself. . . . I will question you, and you shall answer me. Where were you when I laid the earth's foundation? Tell me, if you understand" (38:2-4). And God goes on with his own questions for Job for more than one hundred verses. Job eventually realizes that he is in the wrong and repents: "My ears had heard of you but now my eyes have seen you. Therefore I despise myself and repent in dust and ashes" (Job 42:5,6).

That said, the command to love in Deuteronomy seems incongruent with loving feelings. To me, it sounds more like a demand for submission. So what is God's intention with these words?

Tackling this question was going to take some caffeine. Coffee shops are often full of friends pondering deep philosophical questions, and on Friday mornings during my 180, Sarah and I were among them. We brought our Bibles, our journals, and our questions to the table. Sarah asked a question of her own: "What if God is not so much *commanding* as he is *describing* the kind of relationship he wants with his children? What if we start there?"

This set the tone for our study of the "greatest commandment." We began looking at this passage as a description of the relationship God wants with his children, starting with the people of Israel back in Deuteronomy days (see sidebar "Who Were the People of Israel?") and continuing through human history, all the way to present-day Sarah and me.

We parsed the words from Deuteronomy chapter 6:

Love the LORD your God.

What if the meaning of the verb "love" here is not referring to emotion but rather *devotion?* The Lord in his wisdom knew that the people of Israel were moving into a land where their neighbors would offer them many other gods to love. He didn't want to share their love with the stone and golden statues their neighbors prayed to and worshiped. It's as if he were saying, "Don't give your neighbors' idols even a sliver of your thoughts, even a corner of your heart, even the briefest whispered prayer from your soul, even a few minutes of your strength. Our relationship has absolutely no room in it for flirting with other religions or gods." He wanted all their love, their total devotion. They were that dear to him. And since God knows that all the other gods of the world are imaginary and empty of any power, it was for their own good that the Israelites stick with him.

Love **the LORD** your God.

The use of the term "the LORD" in this passage is significant. In Hebrew, this appears to be God's proper name, perhaps pronounced something like "Yahweh." He explained his name to Moses in Exodus 3:13-15—calling himself simply "I AM" (or "he is" when we use the name Yahweh). "I AM" seems like a mysterious and incomplete name. But when you stop and think, the name really captures what God is saying about himself: He is eternal; he is indescribable; he is unchanging; he is not bound by human language and descriptors. He simply *is.* (Jesus refers to himself by the same name at the end of John chapter 8, and the Jews were ready to stone him for claiming to be God.) "This is my name forever, the name you shall call me from generation to generation" (Exodus 3:15). This same name is used in the Old Testament whenever God wishes to express himself as the faithful, unchanging God who loves his people and keeps his promises.

He wants his people to recall his acts of love and protection, and he wants them to respond with willing devotion.

Love the LORD **your God.**

The phrase "your God" indicates that a relationship already exists. The Israelites had a special relationship with God because he had been preserving and protecting them like no other nation since the days of their ancestor Abraham. He had preserved Jacob's family from starvation in Egypt, watched over the family as it multiplied, led the burgeoning nation out of Egypt in spectacular fashion, provided sustenance in the form of miraculous manna-bread at regular intervals in the desert, and given them a leader (Moses) with a direct line to his heart. God also made sure that his people were unique among nations: He provided a system of regulations to shape their habits and behavior, and he organized their tribes to have various responsibilities to be handed down through the generations. Why did God do all of this? They were special to him. He loved them. They were part of his plan to restore all humankind to perfection. As such, he needed to preserve them and set them apart from other nations who did not know him or acknowledge him as God. Before God's people entered the Promised Land, Moses spoke these words we're studying in Deuteronomy chapter 6. God's overarching message: "Remember what I've done for you" and "Remember who you are."

Now, I am not of Jewish descent, and you may not be either. So how exactly does Deuteronomy apply to us? Well, there was a reason God set the nation of Israel apart from all others: so that his plan of salvation for all people could take place. At the right moment in history, God's Son Jesus would be born to an Israelite human mother who revered him and trusted in his plans. "From now on all generations will call me blessed," Mary said when she learned of God's plan (Luke 1:48). Jesus would grow up to preach and do his miracles among the Jewish people, who had been waiting for him for centuries. Jesus' handpicked missionaries (the twelve apostles) were all Jews, but they did not share the news of Jesus only with their own people. They spread the news about Jesus far and wide. Now "the LORD" of Deuteronomy is *my* Lord because I am one of his children too. The apostle Paul describes this special adoption in his letter to the Galatians: "In Christ Jesus you are all children of God through faith" (3:26). Yes, Deuteronomy is a historical account of the preservation of God's people—a special people through whom the Savior Jesus would be born. But God's children of all times and races find in it a solemn calling to remember who God is, what he did on our behalf, and who we are because of him.

I remember studying Bible history as an elementary school kid, and I often thought that the people of Israel were ridiculous because they constantly rebelled and repeated the same rebellion over and over again. I daresay I may have even thought myself a bit better—more enlightened—than they were because I certainly would never worship a golden calf (Exodus 32), complain about delicious food provided for me (Numbers 11:4-6), or forget about all the amazing miracles he did during my lifetime. Yet here I am, in the middle of my own journey, entertaining Rebellion myself. I've essentially forgotten the significance of what God has done for me, and I'm failing to lead a life of thankfulness.

In these early days of my 180 journey, I prayed that the Lord would help me remember and appreciate what he has done for all humankind, including me. I asked that he would soften my rebellious heart. I prayed that he would replace any feelings of rebellion with feelings of thankfulness.

God answered my prayer. That's when I ran into Mr. Haferman.

YOUR TURN:

- God told the people of Israel that there was no room for any other gods in their relationship with him. He wanted their total devotion. What stands in the way of your total devotion to God?

- Think of a time when you looked to someone or something other than God to get you out of a jam. How did that turn out?

- God wants a loving relationship with his children. How do you think God feels when we rebel against him?

- Have you ever offered your total love and devotion to someone else, only to be rejected? What did that feel like?

Who Were the People of Israel?

There are a lot of stories and seemingly extraneous details in the Bible's Old Testament that could cause readers to question its value. After all, for Christians, all the real action happened in the New Testament, when Jesus entered the world, right? Yes, the Psalms have some good prayers. But the rest is just trivia of who begat whom, rules for eating, and the proper ways to sacrifice a firstborn mammal, right?

It's true that many of the Old Testament laws are not binding for us as New Testament Christians. That's not to say they aren't valuable or true; it simply means they were given for a specific purpose that is no longer relevant after Jesus came to earth. At the same time, if we can see past the laws and genealogies, the Old Testament is an epic account of a God whose love never ran out of steam, even as his love went largely unrequited over the course of four millennia.

Let's review the cast of characters for this Old Testament "biopic," if you will:

EVE: She and her husband, Adam, have the distinct honor of being the first human beings to walk the earth. But their actions spoil the world and doom all humankind to death. Still, God promises Eve that one of her descendants will save the human race.

NOAH: Most of the people around him are following the evil inclinations of their own hearts rather than remembering God and his promise. Noah listens to God and, as a result, many people call him crazy. The colossal ship Noah builds under God's direction saves his family and many living creatures from a devastating worldwide flood. God reiterates the promise of a Savior to Noah and his family too, punctuating that promise with a visual sign—a rainbow.

ABRAHAM: Named "Abram" at first, God tells him to leave his home and journey to a new land where God would make him into a great nation. "All peoples on earth will be blessed through you," God promises (Genesis 12:3). Abram was childless at the time, but God changes Abram's name to Abraham (which means "father of many") and eventually gives him a son in his old age—Isaac.

JACOB: Isaac's son, also known as "Israel." Jacob and his family must flee to Egypt to escape a famine in their homeland. In Egypt they live under the protection of Jacob's son Joseph (of technicolor dreamcoat fame). The Israelites flourish in Egypt— so much so that the Egyptians take notice and begin to fear rebellion from within. The Egyptians enslave Jacob's descendants and treat them harshly.

MOSES: Born to an Israelite woman at a time when Egyptian fear of the Israelites is so intense that the Egyptian king orders genocide: Every boy born in the nation is to be thrown into the Nile River. Moses' mother puts him in the Nile, in a floating basket that is found by the king's daughter. The princess raises Moses in the palace, perhaps affording him the kind of education and experience he would later tap to lead the Israelites out of Egypt.

THE ISRAELITE ENSEMBLE: Often fickle and very expressive, this ensemble follows Moses on the journey back to the homeland that Jacob had left a few generations earlier. As they journey, they camp among settlements of other people who have their own gods and their own ways of living. God gives Moses laws to keep the Israelites safe, separate from distractions, and close to him on the journey. The average Israelite can recite what these laws are—what to eat and what not to eat, when and how to worship, who to marry and who not to marry. God knows it is tempting for them to try out the gods or the routines of their interesting neighbors, or to rationalize marrying the nice boy from one of the nations next door. That's why God insists on total devotion.

There is a huge supporting cast of characters beyond these, all bound together by bloodlines and God's promises. Even through decades when all but a few hundred families deserted God for their neighbors' idols, those few hung on to God's promises and kept waiting for the Savior. The story of the people of Israel is the story of God working through his children and pointing toward his ultimate solution, Jesus. *Remember that point.* We'll explore it more a few chapters later because, as I learned during my 180, it is very relevant for Christians today.

Mr. Haferman

"Let the message of Christ dwell among you richly as you teach and admonish one another with all wisdom . . . with gratitude in your hearts."
—Colossians 3:16

He can be found looking over a practice field fence or watching a concert, observing kids who are not his own but are his by virtue of his calling as a teacher. As I approach him, I can still smell the sweet aroma of his pipe, even though he quit that habit years ago. His smile, his raspy voice, and that sweet fragrance mingle to form a vivid memory of my years as his student.

"Mr. Haferman," I announce as I approach his range of hearing. He turns and gives me that smile. There is something in his eyes that snaps me to attention. Still, after all these years, he is capable of motivating me to present my very best self.

Mr. Haferman is the writing and composition teacher at the Christian high school I attended. (I still remember writing the five-paragraph essay we were required to write for him junior year with the thesis "Love is like an orange.") He has been teaching at this high school for 37 years. Most of the teachers I had in high school are now retired.

We engage in pleasant conversation, both of us gazing out over the football field where my alma mater's current students are playing the first football game of the season. My children are now his students. I told him that I am so grateful my kids have the opportunity to have him as a teacher.

"I'll never retire," Mr. Haferman asserted, his mouth curving up ever so slightly at the edges. His blue eyes danced, and he applauded at something happening on the field. "I'll go on teaching forever, until the Lord calls me home."

"I'm grateful for every day," he said. He pointed to the top of the hill in the distance, where the county highway unfolded toward the high school campus. "Every morning when I reach the crest of that hill and see the campus in front of me, I'm incredibly grateful. What a privilege it is to teach here, to be part of this wonderful Christian ministry, to shape the next generation of leaders. I'm so incredibly thankful."

God put Mr. Haferman in my path on this day so that he could paint this picture of gratitude for me. My teenagers' busy lives require me to drive to the high school nearly every day, often multiple times a day, often in a rush. Now, because of Mr. Haferman, I say a prayer of thanksgiving every time I reach the crest of that hill and the campus comes into view. Mr. Haferman is another gift from God to soften my rebellious heart and remind me of my many blessings.

Indeed, Mr. Haferman, it seems you will go on teaching forever, as your words live on in my heart and as I have the privilege to write them down for others.

YOUR TURN:

- Is there someone in your life who lives thankfully? What can you learn from that person?
- What role does gratitude play in deepening your love for God?

What God Did

"The thing worse than rebellion is the thing that causes rebellion."

—Frederick Douglass

I had not planned on studying Adam and Eve in my 180 study plan. It soon became clear, however, that understanding Rebellion required an understanding of her mission: rebellion against God. I needed to revisit the scene of the crime—the original crime of rebellion against God.

The story from Genesis chapters 1–3 goes like this:

God creates Adam and Eve and gives them the meaningful work of caring for his pleasure-filled creation. He gives them one rule: "Do not eat the fruit from a certain tree in the Garden of Eden; this is how you will show your love for me." Satan, a fallen angel who wants to ruin God's creation (and especially ruin God's beloved children), takes the form of a serpent and leads Eve to doubt that God wants what's best for her. Eve eats the forbidden fruit. She gives a bite to Adam. There are severe consequences for this deliberate act of defiance: Imperfection enters the world in the form of weeds, pests, disease, aging, and eventual death for all living things. What's worse, every human being born to Adam and Eve passes their self-absorbed hearts and imperfect bodies on to the next generation. . . . There are no more daily walks with God within the perfect garden. . . . The holy and eternal Creator has to separate himself from the creatures who were once the crown of his creation but are now flawed and mortal, their hearts opposed to God. God drives Adam and Eve out of the perfect garden, but not before cursing the serpent and promising that victory over Satan's cruel, temporary triumph would come from one of Eve's own descendants.

The story of Adam and Eve, the fruit, and the serpent has reached an almost mythological status in American culture today. Many people understand the references, yet a 2014 survey revealed that less than half of all Americans believe that Adam and Eve were real people ("God's Work? A new poll suggests Americans aren't so confident in their creationism," slate.com, posted December 4, 2014). I am one of the believers: I believe that the Bible is true and gives a historically accurate account of human history. Even if you harbor doubts that the story is true as told, perhaps we can agree that the human condition is flawed.

We and everything around us are mortal and dying. Our flawed condition causes us to search for an antidote.

What is the antidote?

The Beatles would say, "Love is all you need." In other words, live a life of love and that will fix most everything.

Well, let's try that. Imagine for a moment that Jesus, the Savior promised to mother Eve in Genesis 3:15, is not the antidote for the flawed human condition. Imagine a slightly skewed version of our Garden of Eden story. Let's imagine that God wrapped Adam and Eve in his love, but he didn't promise a hero, a Satan-crushing descendant. He just ushered them out of Eden, telling them, "Love is all you need." Here's how that story might go:

Eve eats the forbidden fruit. She gives a bite to Adam. There are severe consequences for this deliberate act of defiance: Imperfection enters the world in the form of weeds, pests, disease, aging, and eventual death. What's worse, every human being born to Adam and Eve passes their self-absorbed hearts and imperfect bodies on to the next generation. There are no more walks with God in a perfect garden. The holy and eternal Creator has to separate himself from the creatures who were once the crown of his creation but are now flawed and mortal, their hearts opposed to God. God drives Adam and Eve out of the perfect garden, saying, "Always remember that I love you, and I want you to love me back. I'll show my love for you by caring for you. Look around and you'll see that I'm always there, providing enough good to balance out the bad. If you stay close to me, you'll get better and better at loving me. You will see love triumph, and that will bring you joy. Ultimately, those who love me will be with me forever. Encourage one another with these words." God's love envelopes Adam and Eve as they leave the garden, sidestepping thorns and swatting mosquitoes. Eve looks up at the powerful angel guarding the entrance to the garden and wonders, "How could God do this to us? Does he really love us? And what if we don't 'get better at loving' him? We couldn't keep loving him when we were perfect. . . . Why should we be any better at it now?"

If the story of Adam and Eve had played out this way, the command in Deuteronomy chapter 6 to love God would look and feel very different. Continuous improvement would be the goal, but how would I know when I achieved enough? A peaceful conscience would depend on my ability to remember God's love, feel it, reciprocate it, and keep improving at it all, even as I experience thorns and pests and tragedies all around me. What's more, reciprocating God's love would mean that I have an important role to play in maintaining my relationship with God, even when God's actions don't make sense to me—even when I step on a thorn and a curse word escapes my lips.

No, if love—human love for God that we somehow coax out of our own crooked hearts—is all we need, then no human being would know true peace of mind. When life is smooth, we might think we love God alright. But what about when God allows someone or something to knock us down flat on our faces? Will we love him then? What about when we remember the reasons he has to be angry with us? Will he seem lovable then? And make no mistake: He has reasons to be angry. God was truly hurt and grieved when Adam and Eve spoiled themselves and their beautiful world. God cursed the serpent, who played a role in the deception. He allowed the weeds and pests and pain and suffering to affect people's lives, including the lives of his children, whom he loves. Some people think of these calamities as a punishment for sin, although we know from the Bible that that's not the case. (See sidebar "Does a Loving God Allow Tragedy?") Some people have trouble loving a God who would allow tragedies to happen. *"How could he do this to us? Does he really love us? How can we love him when he lets us hurt so much?"*

Now, I can't say that I've lived a tragic life, and that's why it has been hard for me to love God more. Sure, there have been tragic and trying events in my life. But those haven't seemed to be my biggest stumbling blocks to loving God more. You'll recall that at first Rebellion used the gnawing question, "Why love God more?" That's how she taunted me. Rebellion's strategy with me was the same strategy the serpent used with Eve—questioning God's authority, his plan, his good will for his children. That was my first stumbling block, and there would be more to come on my 180 journey. (Note that your stumbling blocks might very well be different from mine.) As you'll read later, questions like *Where do I find the strength to love him?* and *Do I love enough?* also were stumbling blocks during my 180.

Actually, these are the exact same questions with which Martin Luther famously struggled five hundred years ago: *Why love God? Where can I find strength to love him? Do I love enough?* Once again during my 180 reflection time, I found myself drawing upon and revisiting some of that head knowledge from my previous studies of Christians who have gone before me. You might appreciate, as I did, some of what Luther learned and shared about his journey toward loving God more.

All his growing-up years and well into young adulthood, Luther had been taught to fear God's wrath, to be uncertain of God's love. And he wasn't alone—most Christians at that time felt the same way. Their church taught them two paths to gain God's approval and favor: confession or a convent. Luther tried them both. Joining a convent (or monastery), he became a friar, vowing to live the rest of his life in poverty, celibacy, and complete obedience to his monastic superiors. But he still felt too sinful for God. So he spent hours confessing his sins, real and imagined, to his advisor in the convent. Then, to make up for his sins, he did penance: He fasted, beat himself, and spent long hours in prayer—sometimes until he passed out from exhaustion. None of this gave Luther any more confidence before God. Nor did it warm his heart with love for God. Rather, this is how Luther described his heart during those years:

> I did not love, yes, I hated the righteous God who punishes sinners, and secretly, . . . I was angry with God. . . . I raged with a fierce and troubled conscience. (Martin Luther, *Luther's Works.* Vol. 34. St. Louis: Concordia Publishing House, 1960, pp. 336–337)

The more Luther tried to manufacture his own love for God, the more it backfired. The deeper his frustration with God, the longer Rebellion's visits became. (I can relate. And all I gave up for God was a slightly earlier bedtime or a little time for housework each night.)

Then Luther rediscovered a truth that had been fading to near extinction in Christian circles before the Reformation period: Christian love isn't about what I do for God; rather, it's about *what God did for me.* God did not simply infuse love into the human condition and, as a result, overlook our sins; he compensated for our sins through sacrifice. Someone needed to pay for the fall into sin, but it wasn't Adam and Eve. Even before the fall into sin, God had an antidote for rebellion in mind. He would act decisively to restore perfection through sacrifice. The Sacrifice would be a descendant of Eve and also God's own son—Jesus. He gave of himself to be the solution. *Agapao.*

God sent his own Son to die on a cross—the sacrifice to pay for the sins of all humankind. Payment made. Peace restored. An angry, brokenhearted God appeased. Jesus gave his righteous life for us, and that became our righteousness. The Bible calls this "atonement"—a complete payment for sin that makes the sinner "at one" with God once again. *"This is how God showed his love among us: He sent his one and only Son into the world that we might live through him. This is love: not that we loved God, but that he loved us and sent his Son as an atoning sacrifice for our sins"* (1 John 4:9,10).

Through Jesus, God showed us what love really is. Jesus left his heavenly home to take on human flesh with me and for me. And talk about self-denial. The King of heaven suffering the death of a slave. The glorious one insulted and naked on a cross by the busiest road into town. The owner of all things living in homeless poverty. The grower of all grains and bestower of all rains (Deuteronomy 11:13-15) suffering hunger and thirst beyond normal human powers to endure. And through it all his Father in heaven watched, saying to the world, *Can't you see how much I love you?*

John 3:16 became one of Martin Luther's favorite portions of the Bible: "God so loved the world that he gave his one and only Son, that whoever believes in him shall not perish but have eternal life." Not a world trying to figure out how to love God, but God loving a world that can never seem to figure it out. That's the eye-opening truth that Luther rediscovered, and it changed everything for him. Here is how he described this love of God, preaching on John 3:16-21 in the year 1532:

> If God had shown the customary courtesy to the world by bidding it a friendly good morning, His attention would certainly have been more than enough. Instead, He goes on to love the world . . . full of wicked, shameful people who misuse all creatures of God in the most disgraceful manner. . . . These shameful people God loves. This is love supreme. . . . He must really be a good God, and His love must be a great, incomprehensible fire, much greater than the fire which Moses saw in the bush, nay, much greater

than the fire of hell. Since this is God's disposition toward the world, who would now despair? This love is too sublime. I cannot do justice to it. I cannot enlarge upon it nor treat it as exhaustively as its reality and truth deserve. (Ewald M. Plass, *What Luther Says*, #2546)

During my 180 journey, as I spent more time in God's Word, I came to realize that I had lost appreciation for God's love *for me*, God's self-denial *for me*, God's sacrifice *for me*. I can't just try harder to love God and close the chasm that necessarily exists between me and God. The stories of Adam and Eve and Luther remind me that loving God more has never been and could never be about gaining God's approval or achieving some kind of fix for this world that we humans wrecked. I need atonement. I need someone to pay for my sins, and not just when I'm feeling as though I need it. I need it because my sin separates me from God and renders me spiritually dead. God demonstrated his love for me with decisive and objective action on my behalf. And I'm quite sure Jesus' motivation to do this for me and all humankind was not some fickle feeling of affection. Pastor Mark Jeske describes it best in his commentary on the topic:

> God's love is different from Hollywood love. TV and movies present love as a mysterious emotional force that you simply respond to and that must be obeyed. When that mysterious force fades away, you no longer need to feel any attachment or obligation to the other person. God's love is more a decision of the mind than an emotional reaction. It is cerebral, not glandular. Jesus chose to take on our flesh, but not because he was enchanted by the fun of childbirth in an animal pen. Jesus chose to make a personal atonement for our sins, but not because he felt like experiencing nails and thorns. (The People's Bible, *James, 1,2 Peter, 1,2,3 John, Jude*, p. 256)

This is love.

God would do that for me? He most certainly would, and did. How could I not feel gratitude? He has freely extended his grace to me, and I have failed to remember that although salvation is free to me, it was not without a price. What's more, God has put me in a time and place where

I can freely hear his Word and grow in his grace. My *head* knew these things; how had my *heart* become so disengaged and disinterested?

As I journeyed further into my 180, the Word worked on my heart. I began to feel something growing in its cold chambers. It was faint at first, and then it began to grow stronger. It was that nagging feeling you get when you know something is not right between you and someone else and you'll do anything to help that person understand how much you wish you could change things and make them right again. It was the feeling that goes along with the words, "I'm so sorry."

(My catechism calls this "contrition." But let's not ruin the moment with head knowledge.)

It wasn't a warm, fuzzy feeling, but it was a start. It was evidence that my heart could feel something other than rebellion. And for this progress I felt something else: *grateful*.

YOUR TURN:

- Read Genesis 3:1-7. What did Eve hope to achieve in her rebellion against God?
- What did Martin Luther hope to achieve with his acts of penance?
- Think of a time when you were angry with God. How did you express that anger? What did you hope would change?
- Have you ever loved someone enough to sacrifice something very important for them? Did that person thank you for your sacrifice? Conversely, has anyone done this for you? Were you thankful?

Does a Loving God Allow Tragedy?

I've had some experience with this question. On January 2, 1998, both of my husband's parents were killed by a semitruck driver who carelessly missed a stop sign and barreled through an intersection.

What did Ted and Judy do to deserve this fate? What did my husband and our family do to deserve such heartache in the aftermath of that tragedy and for years to come?

Actually, the Bible tells us that troubles and heartache and calamity are not God's punishment. (Insofar as they are evil, they don't come from God at all—they come from the wicked hearts of the devil and sinful people.) One reason God allows tragedies is to remind us that this world is not heaven and that we human beings are just as messed up as this world is. We are not fit for heaven. We are separated from the perfection of God. We need a solution to restore us to God again. That solution is Jesus. In him the relationship is fully restored. "The punishment that brought us peace was on him," Isaiah wrote (53:5). Yes, there are hardships and trials in the lives of Christians and non-Christians. God has all of them under his control, serving his purposes. Punishment is not one of those purposes.

(If you want to read a good story about why God allows trouble, read about the man born blind in John 9:1-11. God worked through this man's troubles to draw attention to Jesus, to display his power over everything that afflicts human beings, physically and spiritually.)

Jesus restored the potential for us to have a peaceful, loving relationship with God. A peaceful conscience becomes ours through faith in him, no matter what troubles we face. If your "stumbling block" is understanding why a loving God allows trouble in your life, I urge you to read the Bible verses I read over and over again when troubles hit home:

> Who shall separate us from the love of Christ? Shall trouble or hardship or persecution or famine or nakedness or danger or sword? No, in all these things we are more than conquerors through him who loved us. For I am convinced that neither death nor life, neither angels nor demons, neither the present nor the future, nor any powers, neither height nor depth, nor anything else in all creation, will be able to separate us from the love of God that is in Christ Jesus our Lord. (Romans 8:35,37-39)

Repentance

"Now I am happy, not because you were made sorry, but because your sorrow led you to repentance."
—2 Corinthians 7:9

She had always been a part of my life, but I'm not sure that I kept up with her as I ought to have. Repentance was like one of my 512 Facebook friends: I was acquainted with her, and I could learn a lot from her if I took the time. But it was easy to scroll past her too. Take her for granted. I assumed she would always be there on my list of acquaintances.

Much like Rebellion, Repentance would drop by from time to time, uninvited. I would be sitting in my reading spot, reflecting on God's Word, and suddenly she'd be sitting there with me. She had a knack for knowing exactly when I needed her. Perhaps I was having one of those days when nothing was going right and I had an inkling that it was the result of my poor choices. Repentance knew just how to help with that. Or perhaps it was one of those days when Rebellion was visiting and I really wanted her to go away. Repentance would stop in and Rebellion would sense it was her time to go.

Our conversations were always heartfelt and often led to tears—first tears of sorrow over shortcomings, then tears of joy over restoration. I confess that I had a way of avoiding Repentance if I saw her coming. Sometimes I simply didn't have time for long conversations and tears. I rationalized that I could invite her back another time. Repentance was one of those friends who was always available. Perhaps I took advantage of that.

Repentance knew me well. During one of our visits, she reminded me that we had met years ago—in fact, it was January 25, 1971.

"You realize, I was very young back then," I chuckled. "You have an amazing memory!"

"It was at your baptism," Repentance continued. "I was there to see you brought into God's family, as his own dear child. And because I was there, I can remind you of it whenever you need reminding."

She went on to tell me about that day. "It was beautiful. God put life into your stone-cold heart and ignited a flame of faith (see Colossians 2:9-12). I've seen that faith grow in your heart through the years. You are very blessed."

"I appreciate your stopping by," I said sheepishly. "You always seem to know when I need you." She had a way of restoring joy.

"I'll come by again," Repentance said. "And by the way, you don't have to invite me. Your heavenly Father prompts me to drop by. He knows when you need me."

The more Repentance visited, the more I wanted her to visit. Those were special encounters. I didn't worry whether my house was in order or whether I felt like having a visitor or not. My heavenly Father was in charge of this relationship, and it felt good. I was thankful.

"I feel better after you visit," I admitted to Repentance one day.

Repentance looked intently at me for a moment. "You realize, my dear, that God did not send me to you so that you feel better. That's not his intent."

I asked the obvious question. "Well, then, why did he send you?"

"He sent me so that his holy name would be honored. I notice that many times after we visit, you give thanks to God and your spirits are lifted. Others see that and want what lifted your spirits for themselves too."

"You mean 'who' lifted my spirits," I said.

"Exactly," Repentance said, knowing I understood.

Things looked different after every visit with Repentance. And they began to *feel* different.

Whose Turn Is It?

Repent is a churchy-sounding word that essentially means "to feel regret." The definition I remember from catechism class adds an element of action to the feeling: "to turn away from sin." Sometimes if we just want to talk about the feeling itself, we use another churchy word: *contrition*. Then the whole process of turning away from sin is described by the word *repentance*.

The next logical question is, *Where do I turn?* Turning *away* from sin implies that I turn *toward* something—or someone—else. The apostle Peter, speaking to a crowd in Jerusalem shortly after Jesus ascended into heaven, gave the answer plainly: "Repent, then, and turn to God, so that your sins may be wiped out, that times of refreshing may come from the Lord" (Acts 3:19).

Repentance isn't something we human beings naturally feel in our hearts or can do on our own. "Every inclination of the human heart is evil from childhood," God says in Genesis 8:21. The apostle Paul reiterates that in Romans, "I know that good itself does not dwell in me, that is, in my sinful nature" (7:18). I was acutely reminded of this during my 180 in my confrontations with Rebellion.

So where does the power to turn away from sin and turn toward God come from? *God has to work repentance in our hearts.* And he really can lead even the coldest, stoniest heart to repent, no matter how addicted to or comfortable with sin it is. How do we know this? God promised this to the rebellious people of Israel, and that promise applies to his rebellious children today too: "I will give you a new heart and put a new spirit in you; I will remove from you your heart of stone and give you a heart of flesh" (Ezekiel 36:26).

King David prayed for repentance after he was caught in a sin with particularly devastating consequences (see 2 Samuel 11,12): "Create in me a pure heart, O God" (Psalm 51:10). He prayed those words in his deepest anguish because he knew *the power to change hearts comes from God.*

Chosen

"Love sought is good, but given unsought better."

—Shakespeare, *Twelfth Night*

Life and career coaches will tell you that to discover your passion in life, it's a good idea to look back into your childhood and rediscover simple pleasures that brought you joy. I thought the same might be true for reigniting passion and emotion in my spiritual life during my 180. On the pages of my journal, I journeyed back to those years in my small Christian grade school, when believing in God seemed simple and questions or doubts did not cast a shadow on my joy.

Memories came flooding back: Phonics on the chalkboard. A "Peanuts" lunchbox. Pastor Graf in his 1980s-style eyeglasses. Doodling in my catechism. Kickball in the parking lot.

And then I remembered another game we played at school recesses when I was a kid: Red Rover. The words "Red Rover, Red Rover, let Angie come over" still echo in my mind and make my spine tingle with excitement. I loved that game. To play, the class formed two teams, and the teams would stand on either side of a great expanse of parking lot. One team would decide who from the opposing team they wished to call over to cross the great expanse at a full-on run. All the team members on the calling side would join hands tightly so that as the opposing player approached, he or she could not break through the line. If the running player broke through, he'd take a player back with him to his side. If she did not break through, she was forced to join the opposing team. The team with the longest line of players at the end of recess won the game.

A chant was used to call over the chosen player: *"Red Rover, Red Rover, let ____ come over!"*

I remember standing there in the line, wondering if and when my name would be called. Anticipation hung in the air. When would I be the chosen one? Would my attempt at breaking through be successful? Often the other team's members chose a player they perceived to be a lightweight, in hopes their line would hold back the force of the runner. It didn't matter to me that I might be chosen because I was considered a lightweight. I loved the challenge, and I always hoped my name was called.

This memory led me to think about the joy of being called, or particularly chosen, for a task. Hearing my name called was special. Perhaps that's why I liked the game so much.

Then I got to thinking that the Bible tells me I am chosen.

The apostle Peter's words to some of the earliest Christians apply to me too: "You are a chosen people" (1 Peter 2:9). Peter goes on to describe why I am special: "Once you had not received mercy, but now you have received mercy" (v. 10). *Mercy* means "compassion." It means that God noticed me, saw how hopeless I would be without him, and got his hands dirty picking me up off the ground and cleaning out my wounds. (Sound familiar? Maybe this imagery reminds you of the parable of the good Samaritan in Luke chapter 10. We'll talk about that a little later.) Yes, just as God chose the Israelites as his special people, God chose me to hear his Word and become his child through faith in Jesus. His Word convinced my heart to depend on Jesus (put my faith in him) for my every worry and need, body and soul. God sees my faith and counts it as my new birth certificate with his name on it. "In Christ Jesus you are *all* children of God through faith," Paul writes (Galatians 3:26, emphasis added). And John adds, "See what great love the Father has lavished on us, that we should be called children of God!" (1 John 3:1).

When, exactly, did this calling happen? It's not like I remember the exact moment with spine-tingling excitement. My catechism tells me that I became a child of God at my baptism, and that was more than 40 years ago when I was a young child. (See sidebar "What Is Baptism and Why Does It Matter?") The Holy Spirit entered my heart at my baptism and planted the seed of faith—a seed that would grow as I heard God's Word in my home, my church, and my school. And here's the most amazing aspect of all of this—a fact I had forgotten: God placed me in a time and place in history where all of this could happen. I was born to Christian parents who brought me to Baptism. I could hear his Word and be nurtured by my parents, pastors, and teachers. This is so easy to take for granted. Not everyone has such blessings! In fact, there are still countless thousands waiting to hear the news that God loves them and that Jesus died for them. There are still more who know the good news and do not have the blessing of a Christian church or Christian friends and family around them to support them in their faith life. And there are those who live in places where it is not safe to utter the name of Jesus. Of those, some are even chosen for another reason—to die for their faith.

And here I am, ungratefully entertaining Rebellion. What a sinful, sorry soul I am. A real spiritual lightweight.

The more time I spent in Scripture during my 180, the more I began to see Rebellion for who she really is: my sinful nature, that hereditary condition of wicked ingratitude passed on to all human beings since Adam and Eve. Rebellion had blinded me, so I had failed to see all this grace and mercy extended to me. She downplayed God's calling and dulled my appreciation for being chosen as a child of God. I needed to confront this reality head-on. Remembering the blessing of my baptism was a good place to start. It was the day God called my name. It was special. And now, more than 40 years later, God was giving me a special gift through my 180 project—the gift of rediscovering the joy of being called by name, of being his chosen child, wholly and dearly loved (Colossians 3:12).

I was nearly 60 days into my 180 when I, Angie Molkentin, Spiritual Lightweight, experienced this breakthrough. I hope you can experience this joy too. You are reading this book right now because God chose you and is giving you the opportunity to grow in your relationship with him. Whether God called your name at your baptism long ago or you are a new Christian or you are somewhere in between—or you're not even sure where you are—God invites you and promises to work in your heart and mine through his Word. "Faith comes from hearing the message," the apostle Paul wrote (Romans 10:17). Not only does God call us; he equips us for the journey.

If you stick with me, you'll see how God used the remainder of my 180 journey to build up my faith, strengthen me, and show me how to love him more. He chose me. Now what was he going to do with me? What am I called to do?

YOUR TURN:

- Think of a time when your name was called for a special honor or task. How did you feel about it?

- Have you been baptized? If so, when was the last time you thought about your baptism and its significance in your life?

- You are reading this book right now because God chose you and is giving you the opportunity to go deeper into his Word. What is your reaction to that?

- God promises to work in your heart through his Word. Is there anything standing in the way of your hearing or reading God's Word regularly?

What Is Baptism and Why Does It Matter?

Some churches, like mine, baptize infants. Other churches make Baptism a decision for older individuals to choose. No matter when you were baptized, or if you are still contemplating being baptized, it's worthwhile to review what Baptism is and what the Bible says about it.

○ Baptism isn't just a ceremony. It has power to save: "Baptism . . . now saves you. . . . It saves you by the resurrection of Jesus Christ" (1 Peter 3:21).

○ The Greek word *baptize* means to use water in various ways, whether that's wash, pour, sprinkle, or completely immerse. (Your Bible might have a footnote on Mark 7:4 that says it's even a word used for getting couches clean.)

○ Baptism is a special rite during which an earthly element—water—is combined with God's Word. It might seem strange that water on the skin could wash unbelief out of the soul, but the power doesn't come from the water. It comes from the Spirit working through the Word and the name of God, spoken over the person getting wet. (Notice the specific mention of water in John 3:5 [connected to the Spirit] and Ephesians 5:26 [connected to the Word].)

○ Jesus introduced Baptism as an important part of a life of faith. He himself was baptized (Matthew 3, Mark 1, Luke 3), and he told his disciples to continue doing it: "Go and make disciples of all nations, baptizing them in the name of the Father and of the Son and of the Holy Spirit" (Matthew 28:19).

○ The Bible says Baptism gives the forgiveness of sins: "Be baptized and wash your sins away" (Acts 22:16).

○ At Baptism, something special happens. The Holy Spirit enters a person's heart and begins nurturing faith: "Repent and be baptized, every one of you, in the name of Jesus Christ for the forgiveness of your sins. And you will receive the gift of the Holy Spirit" (Acts 2:38). Baptism makes a person part of the body of Christ (1 Corinthians 12:13).

○ The Holy Spirit works in people the desire to live a new life according to God's will, not our own will. The Bible calls our own will the sinful nature, and it is not capable of loving God or doing anything he wants us to do. Baptism is the act of drowning the sinful nature: It dies just as Christ died. "Don't you know that all of us who were baptized into Christ Jesus were baptized into his death? We were therefore buried with him through baptism into death in order that, just as Christ was raised from the dead through the glory of the Father, we too may live a new life" (Romans 6:3,4).

○ Christ did not stay dead—he rose. And in the same way, through Baptism, a "new self" arises through the power of Christ. We are now capable of loving God and wanting to do his will. "Count yourselves dead to sin but alive to God in Christ Jesus" (Romans 6:11).

○ Baptism becomes practical for daily life when we remember it regularly. We reenact our baptism when we repent and God resurrects our "new self" through faith in Christ. "In Christ Jesus you are all children of God through faith, for all of you who were baptized into Christ have clothed your-selves with Christ" (Galatians 3:26,27).

TRAVEL TIPS:

By now you see how compelled I am to share explanations in the sidebars about important biblical truths. That's because as I progressed further on my journey, more difficult questions arose, and I needed to remind myself of biblical truths that would address some of my emotion-driven questions. I encourage you to do the same on your own journey.

Like me, you'll need to have user-friendly Bible study tools at your fingertips. Here are some tools I recommend to help you keep your focus:

○ **A website like whataboutjesus.com** can walk you through basic Christian beliefs in a friendly and engaging way.

○ **Luther's Small Catechism** is arranged in a user-friendly way for understanding some of the very basics of what the Bible says about God and our relationship with him. (Looking at the diagrams and notes in the margins of my old catechism brought back memories for me!) A new version of Luther's Small Catechism was recently released in conjunction with the 500th anniversary of the Reformation. You can order a copy at nph.net.

○ **The People's Bible series** is a collection of books that offers easy-to-read commentaries on each book of the Bible. They are written by pastors and teachers who believe that the Bible is God's inspired Word and that the Bible's central message points to Jesus as the solution to the human predicament.

Turning Point

"Therefore, if anyone is in Christ, the new creation has come: The old has gone, the new is here!"

—2 Corinthians 5:17

You might think I'm trying to be cute by introducing Rebellion and Repentance as characters in my story. In all seriousness, that's how it happened. Much to my chagrin, these two characters occupied most of the first few weeks of my 180. You'll recall from the "What I Did" chapter that I prayed to notice other people around me who are good examples of loving God. In the early days of my 180 journey, I wondered if God was going to answer my prayers. I was having trouble noticing examples of people loving God. In fact, I was more prone to noticing the opposite! If church was half-empty on Sunday morning, I'd wonder, *Where are all the people who love God?* If I felt snubbed by a friend, I'd think, *If that person really loves God, she would not behave that way toward me.* It was rather disappointing. I had been expecting beautiful revelations. I wanted to fill my notebook with heartwarming stories and acute observations about loving God. Up until about the 60-day mark, the most frequent encounter I had was that voice inside my head asking, *Why love God more? What's the point?* That's when the voice got her name: *Rebellion.*

I am convinced that my crucial confrontation with Rebellion would not have happened were it not for my 180 project. It would have been easier to go on ignoring her as much as possible. I could have said to myself, *As a Christian I'm not supposed to have rebellious thoughts,* and lived my life without ever admitting those thoughts were there. I might have been secretly proud that I chose this path. I never would have repented of those attitudes, and I never would have rediscovered the feeling of gratitude. I most certainly would not have been in a position to think about how to grow in my love for God or recognize other people who love God. I'd still be asking the questions, *Why love God more? Does he even care if I do?*

When Repentance finally arrived on the scene, I experienced a turning point. Literally. God turned my heart away from Rebellion and toward Jesus through faith. It was beautiful and emotional and unexpected. Repentance revived and made useful again the *head knowledge* I had about what my baptism means for my daily life. The Bible verses and explanations I committed to memory during those childhood years in a Christian day school came flooding back to me in a meaningful and practical way.

> Baptism means that the old Adam in us should be drowned by **daily contrition and repentance,** and that all its evil deeds and desires be put to death. It also means that a new person should daily arise to live before God in righteousness and purity forever. (The Meaning of Baptism for Our Daily Life, Luther's Catechism, 1998)

Back then it was just a memory passage. Now, as a result of these visits with Rebellion and Repentance, I was made to remember the value of "daily contrition and repentance"—feeling sorry and turning to God for the solution. My baptism was more than a ritual that happened when I was a child—it was a representation of what happens every day when I repent: My sinful nature drowns—it's gone! Powerless! I stand before God washed utterly clean of all my guilt. My conscience is clear. And a new person arises with the power of Christ. This new self is grateful to God and seeks to do his will. This new self is not satisfied with the head knowledge of knowing God loves me; it desires to respond out of love for God. (See sidebar "Living Sacrifices.") My baptism was the crucial moment when I became alive in Christ, capable of loving God and of seeking his will for my life. Reliving my baptism every day renews that power for living the Christian life.

How weak I had become by letting my baptism fade in its importance. It had become a relic of my Christian life with no practical importance. Now, whenever I remember my baptism, it's as if God is saying, *Remember what I have done for you. (You are pure.) Remember who you are. (You are my own dear child.)*

The recognition that Rebellion is quelled through Repentance—that was my turning point during my 180 journey. Or, rather, it was *God's turning point in me.* Now I was finally ready to begin studying *how* to love God more.

Living Sacrifices

You'll recall from an earlier chapter that the people of Israel were united by flesh and blood and a promise. They lived unique lives. After God's promise of a Savior was fulfilled in Jesus, the rituals, ceremonies, kosher regulations, and sacrifices that had pointed for centuries to Jesus' coming were no longer needed. The New Testament writer to the Hebrews made this clear when he wrote, "We have been made holy through the sacrifice of the body of Jesus Christ once for all" (10:10). After Jesus, the need for that ancient, unique lifestyle for God's chosen people was gone.

Or was it? New Testament Christians (that is, those of us living after Jesus came into the world) are God's children by faith. "In Christ Jesus you are all children of God through faith. If you belong to Christ, then you are Abraham's seed, and heirs according to the promise" (Galatians 3:26,29). When God calls Christians "a chosen people" and "a holy nation" (1 Peter 2:9), he is calling us to lead unique lives too. He wants us to live lives that show devotion to him, set us apart from others, and point to the Savior—just as the people of Israel had done before Jesus. The unique lifestyle of the people of Israel pointed toward the coming Savior and *what he would do;* our lives point toward the Savior and *what he has done.*

That's why it's worth asking, "How can I love God more?" Living the Christian life is our "living sacrifice," the "true and proper worship" of the God who has called us to be his children (Romans 12:1). "Let us continually offer to God a sacrifice of praise—the fruit of lips that openly profess his name," one New Testament writer said to the Jewish converts to Christianity in the years after Jesus' ministry (Hebrews 13:15). "And do not forget to do good and to share with others," he continued (in verse 16), "for with such sacrifices God is pleased."

Now don't get too hung up on the reference to "pleasing God" here. That's a stumbling block I ran into, as you'll read in the chapters ahead. What's important to remember is that Jesus' life, death, and resurrection were the pivot point in history when the sacrifices of God's devoted children turned from acts of anticipation (involving prized fruits and vegetables and first-born mammals burned up by fire) to lives of service (actions done with hearts on fire) motivated by what we know to be true about God's love for all people in Jesus.

TRAVEL TIPS:

You're halfway done with this book! Hopefully it has not been too long of a haul thus far.

At this stage you might be wondering if you can handle a full 180-day journey. If that's a concern of yours, consider a few alternatives:

○ **Consider shortening the number of days** to 90, 45, or even 30. While it's true there is value in going the full distance, I'm confident God will bless any effort you make to grow in your Christian living.

○ **Try using a devotion book with readings already prepared for you** rather than creating your own study. I created my own because I was challenged to do so and because I wanted to read a variety of authors and Bible passages on the topic of "loving God more." Creating your own study is not essential, especially if it becomes a stumbling block.

○ If you decide to choose a devotion book for your study, I encourage you to **find a book that illuminates God's Word.** The power of a 180 is God speaking to you through his Word while you talk with God in prayer and reflect on all of it in your journal. Each reading should direct you to and through a portion of Scripture. Perhaps you know a pastor or Christian mentor you could ask for a trustworthy recommendation.

HOW TO LOVE GOD MORE

To Love God Is to Be Repentant

"Tears come from the heart and not from the brain."

—Leonardo da Vinci

During my 180 journey, certain portions of Scripture really worked on my heart and helped me understand what it means to love God. I read the story of the sinful woman in Luke chapter 7 early on in my study because Jesus had held her up as an example of someone who had "great love." The story fascinated me because of the incredible emotion shown by the woman in the story. Must loving God produce tears? If so, I was in trouble. Although God was softening my heart, I was nowhere near the emotional state of the woman in Luke chapter 7. Her story goes like this (vv. 36-50):

> When one of the Pharisees invited Jesus to have dinner with him, he went to the Pharisee's house and reclined at the table. A woman in that town who lived a sinful life learned that Jesus was eating at the Pharisee's house, so she came there with an alabaster jar of perfume. As she stood behind him at his feet weeping, she began to wet his feet with her tears. Then she wiped them with her hair, kissed them and poured perfume on them.
>
> When the Pharisee who had invited him saw this, he said to himself, "If this man were a prophet, he would know who is touching him and what kind of woman she is—that she is a sinner."

Jesus answered him, "Simon, I have something to tell you."

"Tell me, teacher," he said.

"Two people owed money to a certain moneylender. One owed him five hundred denarii, and the other fifty. Neither of them had the money to pay him back, so he forgave the debts of both. Now which of them will love him more?"

Simon replied, "I suppose the one who had the bigger debt forgiven."

"You have judged correctly," Jesus said.

Then he turned toward the woman and said to Simon, "Do you see this woman? I came into your house. You did not give me any water for my feet, but she wet my feet with her tears and wiped them with her hair. You did not give me a kiss, but this woman, from the time I entered, has not stopped kissing my feet. You did not put oil on my head, but she has poured perfume on my feet. Therefore, I tell you, her many sins have been forgiven—as her great love has shown. But whoever has been forgiven little loves little."

Then Jesus said to her, "Your sins are forgiven."

The other guests began to say among themselves, "Who is this who even forgives sins?"

Jesus said to the woman, "Your faith has saved you; go in peace."

What is the connection between the woman's emotions and her love for God? The Pharisee in the passage also wondered about this. That prompted Jesus to address the question, and he did so with the story about the moneylender and two debtors. Jesus asked which of the debtors loved the moneylender more. The Pharisee and I both had enough head knowledge to answer Jesus' question correctly—"the one who had the bigger debt."

What had this woman's sinful life been? It was something everyone in the town knew about. Had she been one of the village prostitutes?

Had she left her husband and children for another man? We aren't told. Were her tears from sorrow over her sin? Or from joy over finally finding forgiveness in Jesus? We do not know for sure. But it is clear that she was overcome with emotion in this moment with Jesus.

Jesus pronounced that the woman's faith had saved her. It's important to note that the grace of God accessed through faith was what saved her, not her loving acts. She was not saved because of how much that alabaster jar had cost her. She had put her faith in Jesus to save her. Her loving acts were demonstrations of her faith. Anyone who has experienced the forgiveness of sins will find ways to show love for God, because love is a natural outgrowth of faith (Victor Prange, The People's Bible, *Luke,* p. 87).

Jesus contrasted the woman's loving actions with the lack of action by the Pharisee. Sure, the Pharisee had invited Jesus to his home. But he did not show any reverence, any humble service, or even any common courtesies. His thoughts were only critical of Jesus' choices of company. He thought himself to be a pretty good person because he was hosting such a notable figure in his home. Jesus read his thoughts and found them wanting.

"Whoever has been forgiven little loves little," Jesus said, contrasting the woman and the Pharisee. Those words speak to my heart too. At the beginning of my 180 journey, I might have harbored a little pride that I was taking on such a notable project. I needed the Word to work on my heart, to remind me that despite any actions on my part, I still had a debt. My debt cost Jesus his life. I had little appreciation, very little gratitude, and certainly no tears. Not that tears are necessary. . . . Jesus shows us in this passage that a little reverence and some common courtesy may also be good ways to show love. I would learn this a little later in my 180. At this stage, I was still focused on learning what it would take to be moved to tears.

With more than 60 days gone in my 180 journey, my heart had softened and gratitude was growing. But I still had not made many notes of meaningful examples of people around me loving God. I was starting to wonder when God would answer my prayer or whether I was just really bad at recognizing love in action. Looking back, I can see that God wanted to deal with my heart first—to reacquaint me with Repentance and open my eyes. Just as the Pharisee could not see a crying woman's great love until Jesus patiently explained the gratitude behind her actions, God knew I would not be able to recognize love for God until I learned about gratitude.

When God knew I was ready, he gave me a really, *really* good story. And he kept them coming.

YOUR TURN:

- Does sorrow over sin ever move you to tears?
- David says in Psalm 51:17, "My sacrifice, O God, is a broken spirit." Reflect on this statement.

Roger and Lela

"Every player should be accorded the privilege of at least one season with the Chicago Cubs. That's baseball as it should be played—in God's own sunshine. And that's really living."

—Alvin Dark

When I study the topic of love and pray that God would show me examples of people who love God, should I be surprised when he answers my prayer? Certainly not! And yet I am amazed at the remarkable stories and examples he brought into my life one by one during my 180 journey and the expert way he knit them together to teach me. Only God could weave together two dogs, a mandolin, and the Chicago Cubs to display the power of his love to touch hearts.

I need to preface this story by saying that until recently, I did not really know Roger and Lela that well. I met them when we attended puppy training classes at the farm where they lived and trained dogs for a living. They also kenneled dogs on their property, and after our puppy training classes were over, we saw Roger and Lela once or twice a year—whenever we needed to kennel our dog.

I never knew that Roger and Lela were Christians, but I did know that they did very good work and were an absolute pleasure whenever I saw them. I always recommended them to anyone in need of a dog trainer or a kennel.

That's where a couple named Bill and Susan come in. They are a retired couple with whom our family has built a friendship through the years. Bill and Susan have always been very kindhearted to our children, and as a result, our children have learned a few things about kindness from these friends.

You see, befriending Bill and Susan was a big challenge for our children. Every time we said or did something nice for them, they did more for us in return. If we baked cookies, the container would magically return filled to the brim with the best bakery in the tri-county area. If we gave them a hand with something in the yard, cards containing crisp $5 bills would show up for each of our kids. We soon learned there was no outdoing Bill and Susan. We would simply have to accept their kindnesses, thank them, and keep our eyes open for ways we could initiate kindness ourselves.

Through the years as the friendship formed, the conversations sometimes took a spiritual turn. Bill and Susan learned we were Christians, and they could see how important Christianity was for our family. But they themselves remained uninterested in spiritual matters. "We're not religious people," Susan had told me one day in conversation.

I often thought about Bill and Susan and kept them in my prayers. To me it seemed that they *did* have a religion of sorts—it was keeping the scales balanced, even tipped in their favor. During one particularly deep conversation, Bill told me that at the end of his life, he hopes he will have done more good than bad. This seemed like a very logical approach to life. But I always wondered whether Bill's conscience was at peace. Did he ever wonder, *Have I done enough?*

And so the years have passed; our interactions are seasoned with displays of our family values and those of Bill and Susan, which outwardly seem very much in sync. Our attempts to "out-love" Bill and Susan always fall short, providing many laughs and some great conversations with our kids about what motivates acts of kindness.

The white flag

Bill and Susan fly two signature flags in their yard: One is a yellow flag with a smiley face on it, which conveys their optimism and kindness. The other is a Chicago Cubs flag, which expresses their love for their favorite team. I guess you could say that the Cubs flag expresses optimism too, because until 2016 the Chicago Cubs were the epitome of heartbreak and disappointment, unless you were a true fan who never stopped believing that one day the Cubs would indeed win the World Series. Bill always hoped he would live to see the day.

One summer day in 2016, Bill sauntered over to inquire where we had taken our dog for obedience training. Bill and Susan had a new puppy, and they recalled that we were happy with the trainer we had used a number of years earlier. I provided information about Roger and Lela. Bill thanked me and went back inside to catch the Cubs game on TV.

Fast forward to the autumn of that year: The Cubs were making a run for the World Series, and I called Bill and Susan to wish them luck on their team's postseason run. I also inquired how the dog training was going.

"Very well," Bill reported. In fact, Bill and Susan had struck up a friendship with Roger and Lela.

That did not surprise me. Bill and Susan and Roger and Lela are cut from similar cloth: hardworking, disciplined, kind. Bill told me that Roger played the mandolin and that he, Bill, just happened to have a dusty old mandolin in their attic. Bill and Susan gave their old mandolin to Roger in hopes it could be put to use. I chuckled to myself. Of course Bill would have a mandolin in his attic. And of course he would give it away to someone who could use it. That is classic Bill and Susan.

On November 2, 2016, the Chicago Cubs won the World Series in Game 7, after a 108-year drought. I made a note to give Bill and Susan a call the next day. In true Bill-and-Susan fashion, though, they called me first, putting me on speakerphone.

"Hey, we have to tell you a story," Bill said. "You won't believe this."

I waited to hear a tale about how he celebrated the Cubs' big win or about an old friend visiting with a treasured piece of baseball memorabilia. Bill was full of tales about the old days—when a boy could walk up to Wrigley Field and see a ball game with the change in his pocket. None of that, though. On this sacred day after the Chicago Cubs had won the World Series, Bill told me about his latest visit to the dog trainers. It went something like this:

> Roger and Lela invited us in for coffee. And would you believe it, they brought out the old mandolin! It was all cleaned up and ready to play. And did he ever play it! And the two of them sang—the most beautiful music you ever heard. It was Scripture put to music. I had never heard anything like it before. And the way they looked at each other with such love in their eyes while they sang . . . it was like I had taken a magic pill. I was overwhelmed by something. I can't explain it. There we were in that

living room with these soft chairs and this beautiful music. It was like heaven. Wow.

I could not believe my ears. I expected to hear all about the Cubs. Instead, I was hearing about how God touched the hearts of these two friends of mine in a way I never could have imagined.

"Are they the same religion as you?" Susan asked.

"Why, yes. I believe they are," I answered. "And I believe that was God speaking to your heart through the words of Scripture and song," I added.

The conversation didn't really allow for me to add much more to this witness. I praised God, though, that a door had been opened. There may be an opportunity for more meaningful spiritual conversations in our future. Bill and Susan remain in my prayers every day, this experience having reminded me of God's desire for all people to know about him—how he creates opportunities for Christians to share God's love.

Bill and Susan raised a third flag in their yard that day—a white one with a "W" on it. Since 1937, devout Cubs fans see that flag and know their team won its most recent game. I look at that flag now and think, "Wow." The Holy Spirit works through people like Roger and Lela who love God, giving them opportunity to express their love in their interactions with others. That love touches people's hearts. And when it does, it's a spiritual win. I had a chance to witness God's win! I saw God stir more emotion in a human heart than the 2016 Chicago Cubs could.

Wow.

YOUR TURN:

- Many people share their love for God through music. Why do you think music has such power?

- Think of someone who shares his or her love of God in a unique way or through a unique talent. What can you learn from that person?

- What unique talents has God given you? How can you use those talents to show your love for God?

To Love God Is to Obey His Commands

"Produce fruit in keeping with repentance."

—Luke 3:8

When I prepared my 180 study guide, it was clear that I'd have to spend time studying obedience. Multiple Scripture references tell us that obedience is the evidence of loving God, and none is more prominent than Jesus' instruction to his disciples in the upper room:

> Jesus replied, "Anyone who loves me will obey my teaching. My Father will love them, and we will come to them and make our home with them. Anyone who does not love me will not obey my teaching. These words you hear are not my own; they belong to the Father who sent me." (John 14:23,24)

And a bit later in the conversation,

> "As the Father has loved me, so have I loved you. Now remain in my love. If you keep my commands, you will remain in my love, just as I have kept my Father's commands and remain in his love." (John 15:9,10)

Now some might misunderstand this command and think that obedience to God's commands is a condition for our salvation. We've already learned this is not true. Jesus' obedience was credited to us as our righteousness, and we access that righteousness through faith in him. Here Jesus is describing what a loving relationship with him looks like. If we are "in love" with our God, we will learn his commands and strive to obey them, as evidence of a living faith in him.

Let's imagine for a moment that this isn't the case. Imagine that God subscribes to Bill and Susan's concept of the Great Balance Sheet. What a constant state of unrest that would be! How could my conscience be sure that I have done more good than bad? How would I know whether what *I* thought was good really looked good to God? And what if the bad I've done is far worse than I think it is? For as many times as the Bible speaks of God's love and forgiveness, it also reminds us of God's perfection and holiness. "If you, LORD, kept a record of sins, Lord, who could stand?" (Psalm 130:3).

No, obedience must be understood as something separate from a condition of our salvation. It is a natural expression of our faith. It is something we naturally do after we've drowned the sinful nature in repentance and we're ready to live a new life of faith. Notice the word *naturally*. There are many different reasons to obey someone. Some obedience is reluctant: *I don't want to do what you say, but it's better than having you gripe at me all day long.* That isn't the kind of obedience Jesus is talking about here. The Greek word for "obey" used in John 14:23 is *teros.* (See sidebar "Greek to Me.") Its meaning is "to guard or keep." If I have a cherished possession, I am likely to guard it or keep it safe. If I love and cherish my God, Jesus says I will guard and keep dear my God's commandments and instructions—I will want nothing to rankle his happiness and approval.

As we live a life of obedience, we remain in a beautiful state of love with him—much more pleasant than a constant state of unrest. Jesus' life is an example of how to do this. When he says, "Just as I have kept my Father's commands and remain in his love," he is inviting us to look at his life, his relationship with the Father, and to let his example be our guide. And when we look to Jesus, we see the model of gladly and obediently submitting to the will of God the Father (John 6:38), of talking with him in prayer (John 17), of seeking his will (Matthew 26:39), and of serving others (John 13). Jesus' life is an example of guarding and keeping what the Father established as the first and most important commandment in Deuteronomy chapter 6.

I have many friends who are great examples of loving God more by seeking his will and guarding and keeping his commandments. During my 180 journey, it was my friend Dawn who was most present to bring all these examples to life.

YOUR TURN:

- Ask yourself this question: If obedience equates to loving God more, how am I doing?
- How can you pursue and better understand what obedience to God looks like?

Greek to Me

You may be wondering why I occasionally bring up Greek words and attempt to explain their relevance. I haven't added these references in an attempt to impress or intimidate you. The particular observation about the Greek word for "obey" is inserted in this chapter because I had a note about this concept in the margin of my Bible from a previous study. It was something I pursued out of curiosity and shared with you here.

I'm not an expert in Greek. I rely heavily on notes from pastors who are trained in biblical languages and on reference tools such as the footnotes in my self-study Bible or *biblestudytools.com*. I believe that depth and richness can be extracted from the Bible's words when we explore the languages from which the Bible was translated. It's not a necessity for Bible literacy, just something for the curious to pursue. Praise God for those who are gifted in languages who can help us add layers of depth and richness to our studies of God's Word.

Dawn

"We've got reason to get up, reason to get down. He done traded our sin for joy, and now that joy wants out!"
— "Happy Dance" by MercyMe

Dawn is a busy wife and mother who is best described as a five-foot ball of energy. Her frame is so slight that you wonder how it can hold such a big heart. Her smile is so big and sincere that it literally spreads across the whole width of her face. That smile has to be powered by something very powerful on the inside.

And I know it is. Dawn has a deep love for Jesus, and you cannot have a conversation with Dawn without her expressing that love at some point during your time together. She is one of those people who exudes love for God. I always wanted to be like Dawn in that regard, and I must confess I had given up that hope long ago. I figured I just didn't have it in me—whatever that special quality is that Dawn has.

Dawn is one of those friends who will call me up to go for a walk now and then, just to catch up. I'm thankful for those calls because I'm one of those friends who loses track of time. Before I know it, a month passes or six months pass without seeing a friend who I have every intention of seeing. I have a habit of taking friendship for granted.

Dawn is an occupational therapist, and on one of our walks, she was telling me about her recent job change. The change was tough for her because she needed to learn a whole new therapy protocol for a whole new set of doctors. When she wasn't working, she was studying so she could do a good job in her new role. "Good enough" was not acceptable for Dawn. She had to do her best.

That's the first thing I admire about Dawn—her dedication to excellence. I imagine that everyone who has ever worked with Dawn loves to do so because she is competent and good at what she does. That in itself is godly. Dawn reflects Christ in her excellent work. Jesus modeled excellence, and the people said of him, "He has done everything well" (Mark 7:37). The other thing I love about Dawn is that during our conversations, she always finds a way to insert what she read in today's devotion or what she has been studying during her personal Bible study. This time is extremely important to Dawn, and she does a fabulous job protecting it.

"Oh, Angie, you would not believe how busy it has been at work," she told me as we hit our stride. "Tuesday is my long day, so Monday night I looked at my schedule and we had one patient after another scheduled. I said, 'Oh dear Jesus, help me through this day!'"

(That's another thing I love about Dawn. She prays continuously.)

"So Tuesday morning I got up early and I was tempted to skip my devotion and head right in to work because there is all this paperwork we have to do and if I don't get started, with a full day of patients, I'd be there all night! But I said, 'No, put the Lord first, Dawn. Do your devotion and he will direct your day.'"

Then Dawn jumped out into the walking path in front of me and walked backwards to finish her story, beaming from ear to ear and emphasizing her points with her hands, the way some five-foot-tall, ball-of-energy people talk when they are feeling extremely exuberant. "And wouldn't you know it, we had a patient cancel right in the middle of the day, so I could get my paperwork done! I went into the bathroom and did a little happy dance and praised God: 'Thank you, Jesus, for hearing my prayer!'"

I stopped in my tracks and smiled back at her. "That's super, Dawn. It really shows how keeping your priorities straight is a blessing."

We fell back into a side-by-side cadence and enjoyed the rest of our walk. That day Dawn reminded me about priorities and the blessings that come from putting God first. Head knowledge reminds me that God promises great blessings when his people put him first:

> So if you faithfully obey the commands I am giving you today—to love the LORD your God and to serve him with all your heart and with all your soul—then I will send rain on your land in its season, both autumn and spring rains, so that you may gather in your grain, new wine and olive oil. I will provide grass in the fields for your cattle, and you will eat and be satisfied. (Deuteronomy 11:13-15)

Here, through Dawn, I was seeing a living, breathing example of the blessings God grants to his children and seeing the gratitude and joy that his children exhibit when they receive these gifts. Dawn was so excited that God had answered her prayers that she bubbled over with joy. And she shared that joy with me.

I learned something else from Dawn that day. I learned that I want what she has. I want that kind of effervescent love for my Savior that overflows and brings joy and encouragement to others around me. Roger and Lela have it, and God used it to bless Bill and Susan. Dawn has it, and God is using it to bless me. How could I be that kind of blessing to others?

I don't know what kind of vitamins Dawn takes, if she exercises regularly (other than our walks), or if she's just a naturally energetic person. What I do know is that she is in God's Word every day, and even though she is tempted to set it aside some days, she does not, and she is blessed by it. Where does Dawn get her energy? I'm sure God's Word has something to do with it. In fact, I *know* it does. I'm thankful for Dawn, who never fails to show me what it *feels* like to be in love with God.

YOUR TURN:

- Do you know someone who exudes love for God?
- What can you learn from observing that person's behavior?

TRAVEL TIPS:

During your 180 journey:

○ **Take note of others:** When you encounter someone you think is a good example of loving God, write down what you observe in his or her behavior.

○ **Thank God** for the role model he provided for you.

○ **If you have the opportunity, ask your role model about his or her routines and habits.** Look for behaviors you can adopt that might help you develop the qualities you admire.

To Love God Is to Love Others

"My command is this: Love each other as I have loved you."

—John 15:12

About halfway through my 180 journey, I felt like I was really making progress. (Or God was making progress with me!) Ideas about loving God that once had made me bristle were beginning to make more sense. Regular visits with Repentance and disciplined, intentional study of God's Word were indeed increasing my desire to love God more. I was also beginning to see more examples of people who love God, and I was learning from their behavior.

As I continued my exploration, I arrived back at the "greatest commandment," particularly the second part clarified by Jesus:

> "'Love the Lord your God with all your heart and with all your soul and with all your mind.' This is the first and greatest commandment. **And the second is like it: 'Love your neighbor as yourself.'**" (Matthew 22:37-39)

Jesus then added that everything else in the Bible depends on these two commandments. In other words, if you do not have love for God and if you do not show love to others, nothing else in the Bible matters. The apostle Paul explained this in great detail in 1 Corinthians chapter 13 (see sidebar "The Bible's Great Love Chapter"). "If I have a faith that can move mountains, but do not have love, I am nothing" (v. 2). Nothing! These are some pretty emphatic statements from both Jesus and Paul. That's why I spent a fair amount of time during my 180 journey trying to understand the relationship between loving God and loving others.

I particularly enjoyed digging into the epistle of 1 John because it does a wonderful job of explaining why these two commands—loving God and loving others—are linked. "Dear friends, since God so loved us, we also ought to love one another. No one has ever seen God; but if we love one another, God lives in us and his love is made complete in us" (1 John 4:11,12).

What an awesome thought! People see God's love through us! People can learn about God's love when they read the Bible, but they get to see it, hear it, or *feel* it when we Christians love in his name. That's what C. S. Lewis alluded to when he said Christians ought to be "little Christs" to one another. Luther said it too:

> [A]s our heavenly Father has in Christ freely come to our aid, we also ought freely to help our neighbor through our body and its works, and each one should become as it were a Christ to the other that we may become Christs to one another and Christ may be the same in all, that is, that we may be truly Christians. (*On the Freedom of a Christian*, 1520)

What an incredible responsibility! God loves us perfectly, in fact, "while we were still sinners" (Romans 5:8) and before we were capable of doing anything lovable. That's the model: to love others not because of who they are or what they can do for us but precisely because they are fellow souls loved by Jesus. This isn't easy for us flawed human beings to do. Our interactions and relationships are rife with good intentions gone wrong, misunderstandings, misgivings, and many, many mistakes. We won't fully understand perfect love until we are perfectly transformed in heaven. Nevertheless, we try. We try because "Christ's love compels us" (2 Corinthians 5:14).

That passage goes on to say that because of Christ's love, we no longer live for ourselves but for Christ. Loving others with perfect, sacrificial, Christlike love is difficult. In fact, such discipleship is sometimes compared to carrying a cross as Christ did. "Whoever wants to be my disciple must deny themselves and take up their cross and follow me," Jesus said in Matthew 16:24. Loving others might feel like a cross sometimes—when sin gets the better of us or when we've been wronged. But we're not alone; we have the strength God provides. Pastor Mark Jeske puts it this way:

> Believers love to hear God's will and do it. His commands are not burdensome. His yoke really is easy and his burden really is light. How many heads fit in a yoke? Two, right? Who is pulling alongside you? Jesus, of course. He daily assures us of forgiveness for our failures and gives us strength and stamina for each new day. (The People's Bible, *James, 1,2 Peter, 1,2,3 John, Jude*, p. 259)

Furthermore, the Lord promises blessings to those who find delight in serving him and others. "Blessed are those who fear the LORD, who find great delight in his commands" (Psalm 112:1).

I know many people who love and serve others, and do so joyfully. During my 180 journey, I met a lady named Nan who served as a beautiful example for me of "delightful" love.

YOUR TURN:

- Read 1 Corinthians 13:4-7. Which of these descriptors of love do you find easiest to exhibit toward others? Which do you find most difficult?
- Are there people in your life who are easier to love than others?
- How can Christ's example of love help you as you strive to love others more?
- Is loving and serving others a delight for you? (If yes, praise God for that joy!)
- When it is not a delight, how can you reconnect with the joyful feeling of loving and serving others?

The Bible's Great Love Chapter

If you want to learn more about how to love others, look no further than the Bible's description of love in 1 Corinthians 13:1-13. Here you'll find all the descriptors of what love looks like in action: patient, kind, not envious, not proud, and the list goes on.

In this section of Scripture, the apostle Paul was writing to a group of Christians who had many gifts for serving God and others (Paul calls them spiritual gifts). But these Christians were still relatively immature in their faith life. Paul wanted to help them understand what love looks like in action, and he needed them to see that love is the motivating factor for *everything* a Christian does. To drive home his point, he used very picturesque language and hyperbole:

> If I speak in the tongues of men or of angels, but do not have love, I am only a resounding gong or a clanging cymbal. If I have the gift of prophecy and can fathom all mysteries and all knowledge, and if I have a faith that can move mountains, but do not have love, I am nothing. If I give all I possess to the

poor and give over my body to hardship that I may boast, but do not have love, I gain nothing.

Paul draws some pretty big contrasts here: Even the most angelic voices and prolific preachers sound like clanging cymbals without love. All the head knowledge in the world is nothing without love. Incredible generosity produces no real results without love.

"The greatest of these [gifts] is love," Paul concludes in verse 13. Everything else will fade away, but love has an eternal quality: Love will still be present between God and his children when we leave this earth and join him in the perfection of heaven.

Nan

"Spread love everywhere you go. Let no one ever come to you without leaving happier."
—Mother Teresa

There are some people included in this book simply because a brief encounter with them served to teach me something about loving God more. Nan is one of those people. She is the wife of a friend of a friend, a delightful person I happened to meet once or twice before my 180 journey began. We first met when a mutual friend invited us to a New Year's Eve party. Throughout the evening, I picked up on various conversations and learned that Nan was battling breast cancer. She and her husband Brad have five children, one of whom is on the autism spectrum. When I first met Nan, I thought, "There is a woman with her hands full." I kept her in my prayers.

One year later, and smack dab in the middle of my 180 journey, Brad and Nan invited us and the rest of the gang of mutual friends to their house for New Year's Eve. By this time, Nan had finished her cancer treatments and was finally sporting her own beautiful hair. She welcomed us with a gorgeous smile. As the house began to fill with guests, Nan bustled about as the gracious hostess. From my perch on a kitchen stool, I could not help but notice each of her interactions seasoned with a smile. More ice? Sure, let me get that for you. Oops, a spill? Here is a cloth. I was happy that Nan was doing so well.

There was something about Nan that particularly caught my attention. I mentioned her beautiful smile. . . . Well, each time one of her kids came into the kitchen, her face lit up as if the most important person in the world was standing before her. She was not too busy for them. She was not irritated that they had invaded the adult party space. She listened to whatever had to be said, responded, and the child went away happy. I imagined those children were supremely confident in their mother's love.

Nan certainly had excuses to feel exasperated. She had a house full of people; she was trying to carry on conversations while playing hostess; and she may have been tired from all her body had endured the past year. Yet, she offered that beautiful smile. *Love is patient, love is kind.*

That evening I asked myself whether my face could be arranged into such a delightful smile whenever one of my loved ones stood before me. No matter what I was doing, could I treat that person as if he or she were the most important and precious person in the world at that moment? What a blessing it would be for others to feel God's love through me. I was reminded of the passage from 1 John 4:12: "No one has ever seen God; but if we love one another, God lives in us and his love is made complete in us."

I doubted that I could do it unless I changed some habits:

- I would need to remember how God promises to see *me* when I come to him in repentance: "He will take great delight in you; in his love he will no longer rebuke you, but will rejoice over you with singing" (Zephaniah 3:17).

- I would need to remember that God is the source of all love: "Dear friends, let us love one another, for love comes from God" (1 John 4:7).

- And I would need to ask for an added dose of strength from the power source: "If anyone serves, they should do so with the strength God provides, so that in all things God may be praised through Jesus Christ" (1 Peter 4:11).

That night I gave glory to God for Nan, and I prayed that God would allow me to overflow with love for others.

YOUR TURN:

- When it comes to loving others, do you always show patience and kindness? When is it more difficult to exhibit those qualities?

- Do you know someone who is a role model for patience and kindness?

- What habits might you have to change to exhibit more patience and kindness?

Falling Short

"Do. Or do not. There is no try."

—Yoda

More than halfway through my 180 journey, things were humming along. I was in the Word, and the Word was working on my heart. God also used the examples of other Christians to help me shape my behavior.

- Mr. Haferman modeled gratitude.

- Roger and Lela used their talents to bless others.

- Dawn was bold about sharing how God was working in her life.

- Nan was joyful and patient with those around her.

Yes, God was giving me all I asked for during my 180 journey. I was living most every day with heightened awareness of what loving God means and how I can reflect that love to others. My attitude and my behaviors were beginning to change. And it was all so very peaceful and satisfying.

Until it wasn't.

A new feeling surfaced—*failure*. The more I studied love, the more I wanted to do it—and the more I realized how bad I was at loving God and others as God intends. It was rather unsettling.

Looking back now, I blame one word for bringing feelings of failure to the surface: *must*. Two weeks of my 180 journey were devoted to studying the topic of loving others as a natural outgrowth of loving God more. Sarah and I studied several key portions of Scripture that provided examples of what love looks like when demonstrated to others:

- "A new command I give you: Love one another. As I have loved you, so you **must** love one another. By this everyone will know that you are my disciples, if you love one another" (John 13:34,35).

- "Love **must** be sincere" (Romans 12:9).

- "Love one another deeply, from the heart" (1 Peter 1:22).

- "Dear children, let us not love with words or speech but with actions and in truth" (1 John 3:18).

- "Whoever does not love does not know God, because God is love" (1 John 4:8).

- The parable of the good Samaritan, which illustrates how to demonstrate love through action (Luke 10:25-37).

Studying these portions of Scripture stirred up inside of me a deep sense of inadequacy. My own ability to love God or anybody else was pitiful compared to how I ought to live and what I must do if I am to demonstrate more love for God. What's more, God kept putting people in my life who needed more of my love. Many days I was out of energy, completely tapped out, and feeling guilty that I was not more loving to my neighbors. I actually found myself closing my eyes to the needs around me so that I would not have to add one more thing into my busy day. This too stirred feelings of guilt.

I knew my salvation was not dependent upon my actions, yet I was feeling the pressure to engage, to not pass by on the other side of the road, to not ignore people who need love or attention. After all, Christ died for me that I might serve him. "Those who live should no longer live for themselves but for him who died for them and was raised again" (2 Corinthians 5:15). There was that imperative again: *should.*

I questioned everything as I wrote in my journal: Was my 180 working? Was I becoming more loving? Or simply becoming more aware of my failures? (See sidebar "What's Your Struggle?") I wanted to find a way to show love to others *and* to delight in doing so. Was that possible? I found myself longing for peace.

This was one of those times when I interrupted my regularly planned study of what love looks like and went back to some of the passages that gave me peace. Passages like "I have loved you with an everlasting love" from Jeremiah 31:3. And this one from the book of Psalms:

> The LORD is compassionate and gracious,
> slow to anger, abounding in love.
> He will not always accuse,
> nor will he harbor his anger forever;
> he does not treat us as our sins deserve
> or repay us according to our iniquities.

For as high as the heavens are above the earth,
so great is his love for those who fear him;
as far as the east is from the west,
so far has he removed our transgressions from us.
As a father has compassion on his children,
so the LORD has compassion on those who fear him;
for he knows how we are formed,
he remembers that we are dust.
The life of mortals is like grass,
they flourish like a flower of the field;
the wind blows over it and it is gone,
and its place remembers it no more.
But from everlasting to everlasting
the LORD's love is with those who fear him,
and his righteousness with their children's children—
with those who keep his covenant
and remember to obey his precepts. (Psalm 103:8-18)

Why did I feel the need to go back to these Old Testament promises? First of all, I needed comfort. The prospect of loving others the way God loves me is a daunting task. In fact, it is a standard that can never be achieved, a continuing debt we can never pay off (Romans 13:8). Holding myself to this standard, I should expect to feel resentment, frustration, and fear of failure. The quieting passages of the Old Testament—many of which speak of God's unending love despite his children's failures—speak to contemporary hearts as well.

Second, I needed to remember the reason behind loving others: to be a conduit of God's love (as described in 1 John 4:12, which we discussed in an earlier chapter). To be sure, loving others brought blessings into my life: I enjoyed the peace I felt for doing good and the gratitude I received from others who benefited from my service. God wants us to enjoy those blessings. But he never wants us to forget who the hero of the story really is (not me) and what the real definition of love is (what he does for me).

Consider the story of the good Samaritan from another vantage point:

I am the poor man who was robbed and beaten and left
for dead on the side of the road.

The church passed by and could not save me.

My own good works passed by and could not save me.

Then, the most unlikely person intervened, healed my wounds, paid my debts, and made sure I was cared for. Jesus Christ is my Good Samaritan.

"Go and do likewise," Jesus says.

Yes, there are people who need my pity, who need me to be a neighbor to them, maybe even a little bit of a hero for them. But when that gets overwhelming, here's what I need and want to remember: *Jesus Christ is the hero of my story.* He fulfilled all the "shoulds" and "musts" of God's commands and binds up the cuts and scrapes I receive from trying so hard to do it myself. When I am wounded by my failures, he says, "I got this." Jesus is the perfect love that "drives out fear" of judgment (1 John 4:18). While it's healthy to engage in activities that strengthen us in Christian living (like a 180 journey), it's unhealthy to be driven by the question, *Am I enough?* Jesus paid for my shortcomings. In grateful response, I love with the strength that God provides (1 Peter 4:11). Then God gets the glory for my actions. He's the hero.

Still, I wanted to do it all and feel it all. I wanted to be more like Dawn or Nan or the repentant woman from Luke chapter 7—all of whom exude love. Must I get to that place? Are such emotions the evidence of loving God?

That's when I started thinking about my dad, and I began to see another facet of what loving God looks like.

YOUR TURN:

- Do you ever feel like you are failing in loving others around you?
- What can you do with those feelings of failure?
- How is God using those feelings to draw you closer to him?

What's Your Struggle?

If you try a 180 of your own, you will regularly bump up against your own struggles. In the beginning, I struggled with apathy. At the middle stage, I struggled with a guilty conscience for all my failures. You may struggle with these or other conflicts, such as an inability to forgive, blinding emotions, or a lurking addiction. Each of these challenges weakens our ability to make godly choices.

Understand that there will always be struggle as we strive to live godly lives. Paul describes it this way in his letter to the Galatians: "The flesh desires what is contrary to the Spirit, and the Spirit what is contrary to the flesh. They are in conflict with each other, so that you are not to do whatever you want" (5:17). Paul is describing the everyday struggle within us between that old sinful nature and the new self who wants to live a life of love and service to God and others. We all need the same solution: repentance and the renewal that comes from God.

David reminded us where we can find steadiness when he wrote in Psalm 51:10: "Create in me a pure heart, O God, and renew a steadfast spirit within me." This prayer helped me because it turned me back to the source of all love: God himself. He provides the fuel to love others more and the forgiveness for falling short.

Whatever the struggle is for you, I urge you to use your journal to explore it further. In fact, on a particularly difficult day, open your journal to a blank page. Draw a cross on the page. Then name your struggle and write it down, right at the foot of the cross. "Cast all your anxiety on him *because he cares for you*" (1 Peter 5:7).

Dad

"Always give yourselves fully to the work of the Lord."
—1 Corinthians 15:58

As I have said, my 180 journey included a daily prayer:

- Lord, help me to love you more,

- Give me a better understanding of what it means to love you more, and

- Help me notice other people around me who are good examples of loving you.

The people I first noticed who were good examples of loving God were people who, as Sarah said, "exuded" love. Nan's smile. Dawn's happy dance. Roger and Lela's beautiful music. These were compelling, emotional expressions of love that noticeably overflowed.

Then, at just the right time, I began noticing people who didn't necessarily wear their hearts on their sleeves, yet I knew they had a deep love for God. My dad is a perfect example for me of this sort of person.

Dad is in his early 70s. He is tall and lanky with piercing blue eyes and a smile he gives generously to those he knows and trusts. He was trained as a machinist and, in fact, still works a part-time job in a tool-and-die shop even though he is "retired." (He likes the discipline of getting up every morning and going to work.) In his 20s, Dad gave up his good factory job to pursue his dream of owning his own farm. He bought a dairy farm and, together with my mom, worked extremely hard to make that farm successful during the difficult agricultural economy of the 1980s. The farm *was* successful. It supported our family of five and now has been successfully transitioned to my brother, who is today raising a farm family of his own.

People would often ask my dad why he gave up his steady factory job to work so hard running a farm, with all its uncertainties and risks. Dad liked the work. He liked the challenge. And, more important, he liked to be his own boss. You see, my dad isn't really a "people person." He's an introvert who finds interacting with people very tiring. (He'll be the first to admit that he sometimes says the wrong thing in conversation. And then he'll stew over his mistakes later. I am sure it is exhausting for him.) So in the years when many farms were expanding and hiring employees, Dad was determined to find a way to farm without managing more people.

This same man who would rather spend time with cows and barn cats than people has also been a church council member in various congregations for as long as I can remember. And he's not just the quiet maintenance man at church. The majority of his years of service have been spent as an elder in charge of visiting church members whose attendance has been sporadic or who have seemed to stray from the faith. Arguably, Dad holds one of the most difficult volunteer positions in the church—especially for an introvert who does not think of himself as a man of words.

Why in the world would Dad do this? Where does he get the strength? It's not like an elder who goes after straying Christians receives much glory or reward. It's difficult work. Most people in danger of falling away from the faith really dislike a knock on the door from a church elder, even if that knock is powered by God's love. Dad has had doors slammed in his face and has shown up to many homes where the appointment was "forgotten." He has listened to a litany of complaints that keep people away from church. Those can't be very uplifting conversations.

I had to understand what made Dad act in such a loving way. One day during my 180 journey, I met Dad for lunch and struck up a conversation about his service at church. "You've been doing this elder work for a long time," I observed. "And it's not easy to talk with someone who is disillusioned with church."

Dad seemed surprised that I introduced this topic. Usually we didn't get into deep conversations. But I really wanted to hear how Dad would express his love for God.

"I don't know," he shrugged. "Someone has to do it."

"What keeps you going?"

He shrugged again. "I guess I just like to see what happens."

And then, between bites, he talked about the latest soul he was "working on." By "working on," I knew he meant "encouraging in the faith." And I could tell this "working on" meant very much to him.

I told Dad that I admired him for his persistence and the way he obviously cares about other people. He shrugged. He didn't say it, but I knew that shrug meant: *I am just trying to do what God wants me to do.*

I left our lunch with another story added to the many in my memory of how Dad has "worked on" people in his own steady way. I'm sure many people have snubbed him. But the few who connected on a deeper level did come back to church. The Holy Spirit worked on their hearts, and the words that tumbled from Dad's mouth—awkward or not—never came back empty.

Dad is not someone who exudes love, or even expresses it in words. And yet I know he must have a deep love for God, because very few human beings make it their life's work to put themselves in such uncomfortable positions just to "see what happens." Dad's actions show me that love for God is putting God and his work first, no matter what you think about yourself or how it makes you feel. Dad's elder work is in itself an act of worship, as is every action done out of faith. Dad speaks God's Word and then stands back to see what God does with it. For Dad, God is the hero of the story.

Maybe love for God does not need to be demonstrated with an overflowing of emotion. Perhaps it cannot even be expressed in words. Maybe it is demonstrated by people like Dad who order their lives in such a way that God's work is first above all else. This thought is comforting to me, because trying to exude love—thinking about it all the time—can be exhausting. Trying to be a hero, even if it is in the name of love, is exhausting. Dad is a man who loves God very much but doesn't talk about it. He just does God's work and waits to "see what happens."

YOUR TURN:

- Think of someone you know who shows love for God with action, without a lot of words or emotion. What can you learn from that person?

- Think of a situation where you can serve someone else out of love. Do you have the patience to wait and see what God does with that service? How will you feel if you don't see the results of your work?

- Make a list of your own unique talents and strengths. How might God use you to uniquely serve his purposes?

- Now make a list of your perceived weaknesses. Can you think of a time when God's work was done through you, in spite of those weaknesses?

TRAVEL TIPS:

During your 180 journey:

○ **Give glory to God for those you observe** who are good examples of loving God. Ask yourself what you can learn from each example.

○ If you find yourself falling short of the good examples these people provide, **guard against the temptation to see only your weaknesses.** Rather, view yourself as God views you: his own redeemed child renewed by grace and empowered by Christ to produce God-pleasing fruits of faith.

○ **Be yourself,** and watch what God does through you!

To Love God Is to Put Him First

"We might think that God wanted simply obedience to a set of rules: whereas He really wants people of a particular sort."
—C. S. Lewis, *Mere Christianity*

Most Christians want to do good, and we may get frustrated when we can't live up to God's standards. That's especially the case when you take on a project designed to improve your Christian living. The heightened awareness can amplify the guilt when you fail.

There are beautiful portions of Scripture that are of particular help to well-meaning Christians who struggle in their Christian life of faith. During my 180 journey, a portion of Scripture came to my attention that wasn't in my study plan. This story, together with the example of my dad and countless other quiet Christians like him, shed light on the idea that loving God is not about feelings, nor is it about measurement. It's a way of living. It's just something you do. I'd call it a *mind-set,* but I don't want to give the impression that loving God is something I could set my mind to all by myself. (That would make me the hero of the story.) Perhaps this portion of Scripture from Luke chapter 17 will explain what I mean. It's a section that the NIV 2011 translation calls "Sin, Faith, Duty."

In this story, we read about a standard Jesus set for his disciples—a standard that led to frustration because it seemed unattainable.

> "If your brother or sister sins against you, rebuke them; and if they repent, forgive them. Even if they sin against you seven times in a day and seven times come back to you saying 'I repent,' you must forgive them."
>
> The apostles said to the Lord, "Increase our faith!"
>
> He replied, "If you have faith as small as a mustard seed, you can say to this mulberry tree, 'Be uprooted and planted in the sea,' and it will obey you.
>
> "Suppose one of you has a servant plowing or looking after the sheep. Will he say to the servant when he comes in from the field, 'Come along now and sit down to eat'? Won't he rather say, 'Prepare my supper,

get yourself ready and wait on me while I eat and drink; after that you may eat and drink'? Will he thank the servant because he did what he was told to do? So you also, when you have done everything you were told to do, should say, 'We are unworthy servants; we have only done our duty.'" (Luke 17:3-10)

Jesus set the standard for how his disciples were to love and forgive others, and it was a high standard. When he says to forgive "seven times in a day," he means that whenever someone repents and asks for our forgiveness, we are to give it. The reference to "seven times" underscores just how freely forgiveness is to flow. For example, I may get frustrated with my husband for leaving his socks on the floor every day. By Jesus' standard, my husband could leave seven pairs of socks on the floor at regular intervals throughout a day and, if he is repentant, I ought to freely forgive him without so much as a sigh.

Recognizing this as a difficult standard, the disciples exclaimed, "Increase our faith!" They knew they needed help if they were going to live up to these standards. That, incidentally, is exactly how I was feeling during my 180 journey as I tried to love others the way God loves me. *"Lord, increase my faith! I need help!"*

Jesus' reply to his disciples here in Luke chapter 17 was interesting. He didn't say, "Of course I will help you reach this standard. Thanks for asking." Instead, Jesus directed them away from self-analysis and toward action. He pointed out that any amount of faith has power—even faith as small as a mustard seed (which is really tiny—only 1-2 millimeters in diameter). The key is to use your faith. Live it. Apply it to the situation right in front of you, whenever you have the opportunity. Jesus then went on to talk about the duty of a servant to his master. The servant should not come to his master expecting to be praised for the accomplishments of the day. Rather, he should simply do his duty, trusting the master to see that he will be fed in due time. So while the disciples were introspective and worried about having enough faith, Jesus was saying, "Stop measuring. Just do your work."

This is how my dad lives. The example of my dad combined with this portion of Scripture was of great comfort as I struggled with God's high standards of loving him and others. I learned that people of faith use their faith to love God in different ways. Those expressive people whose emotions spill over for all to see are not the *only* people who love God. If you are not a particularly expressive or emotional person, you can still love God by doing the work he has placed before you. Use what you have. Be who you are. Do the work in front of you. It's all very clear in verse 10: "So you also, when you have done everything you were told to do, should say, 'We are unworthy servants; we have only done our duty.'"

Repent, then go back to work.

This is the way of living for so many strong, humble Christians like my dad who love God. I began to see them all around me during the latter half of my 180. When I engaged in conversation with them, thanked them for their service, or complimented them on a loving act I observed, they demurred with a shrug, not quite sure how to take a compliment for something they were doing simply because they were Christians.

And so this truth became very clear to me: Loving God is ordering your life in such a way that God and his will come first. It's not some kind of balance sheet. It's just plugging away, getting the next thing done, and the next thing, and the next. God's love keeps no record of my wrongs and, therefore, *I* keep no record of my wrongs. I put those wrongs at the foot of the cross every day in contrition and repentance. Conversely, God keeps no record of rights either. When God is first in my life, when I seek his will every day in his Word and in prayer, I'll naturally do more loving things. "Seek first his kingdom and his righteousness, and all these things will be given to you as well," Jesus said (Matthew 6:33). In other words, put God first and he will bless you with everything else you need, including the ability to live your faith. I would soon learn more about the blessings God has in mind for us when we put him first in all things.

Our God is a God of order (1 Corinthians 14:33). He does not change his mind about us (Malachi 3:6). There is something very peaceful and comforting in God's consistent heart for anyone who is struggling with human emotions of any kind. Emotions can be wild and volatile. They can be present one day and fleeting the next. When driven by emotion, we ask questions like, *Why love God more?* or *Am I loving God enough?* or *Am I expressive enough of my love?* Those can be valuable questions for self-improvement, as long as we do not forget that our worth in God's eyes is not dependent on our actions. My acts of love toward others, whether successful or bountiful or eloquent by any measure, are evidence of the love of God (his for me and mine for him) living in me.

Jesus referred to this as "bearing fruit" in his beautiful vine-and-branches analogy:

> I am the vine; you are the branches. If you remain in me
> and I in you, you will bear much fruit; apart from me
> you can do nothing. This is to my Father's glory, that you
> bear much fruit, showing yourselves to be my disciples.
> (John 15:5,8)

Jesus gave us this vivid, physical depiction of what loving God looks like to bring us out of the realm of invisible and emotional and into a Christian life that is visible and tangible to others. This fruit-bearing life happens when we remain in him. In other words, put God first in your daily schedule, stay close to him in Word and prayer, and see all the amazing things he gives you the will to do—as my dad says, "See what happens." After all, that's what God has done, and continues to do, for and through so many people who love him—real human beings with a wide range of talents, personalities, upbringings, experiences, and paths in life. Love, an intangible, becomes tangible through the hands of Christian love extended in dutiful service toward others.

That's what I began to see and appreciate in the latter half of my 180 journey. I began to see how many different kinds of people love and serve God in various ways. And I began to think about who God is—how big he has to be—to have all this under his control.

YOUR TURN:

- How do you put God first in your life?
- What is the work God has set in front of you to do?
- What is your attitude toward that work? Can others see that you love God by the way you perform that task?
- Do you know someone who quietly produces Christian fruit? What can you learn from that person?

Wait for It

During a 180 journey, you are spending time focused on a particular topic. You are praying that God will give you insights, provide examples, and reveal connections you never knew existed.

During my 180 journey, I gradually began to see and appreciate all the people, lives, systems, and laws of nature God has under his control. He was making connections for me that I never could have planned, no matter how organized I was about my 180 journey. He was in control of my 180. It really was amazing.

This heightened awareness stirred a new emotion in me—*awe*. It was something like David expressed when he wrote Psalm 8:

> When I consider your heavens,
> the work of your fingers,
> the moon and the stars,
> which you have set in place,
> what is mankind that you are mindful of them,
> human beings that you care for them? (vv. 3,4)

As my 180 journey continued, it became easier to praise God. I wanted to praise him more because my awe of him was growing. God was working through various means—his Word, people, and prayer—to draw me closer to him. More time in his Word helped me better understand his steadfastness, his control of all things. It took me a while to get to this place.

If you try a 180 journey of your own, be patient and steadfast—the second half of the journey can be really great. "Wait for the Lord," David wrote multiple times in his psalms. Trust that the Lord is blessing your journey. See what happens.

Burning Questions

"We know that in all things God works for the good of those who love him, who have been called according to his purpose."

—Romans 8:28

On a rock-strewn hillside in a lonely desert, a man was minding his own business, tending his sheep. At one point he turned his gaze in the opposite direction and saw a bush on fire.

That's strange. No storm clouds around. And I haven't seen anyone else around here all day.

Time passed.

Wait. It's still burning. It doesn't seem to be burning out. I gotta check this out.

"Moses! Moses!" a voice called.

He gave one swift glance over the flock to be sure all was well, then trekked across a rocky expanse toward the mysterious bush.

"Here I am."

And the story continues, from Exodus:

> "Do not come any closer," God said. "Take off your sandals, for the place where you are standing is holy ground." Then he said, "I am the God of your father, the God of Abraham, the God of Isaac and the God of Jacob." At this, Moses hid his face, because he was afraid to look at God.
>
> The LORD said, "I have indeed seen the misery of my people in Egypt. I have heard them crying out because of their slave drivers, and I am concerned about their suffering. So I have come down to rescue them from the hand of the Egyptians and to bring them up out of that land into a good and spacious land, a land flowing with milk and honey—the home of the Canaanites, Hittites, Amorites, Perizzites, Hivites and Jebusites. And now the cry of the Israelites has reached me, and I have seen the

way the Egyptians are oppressing them. So now, go. I am
sending you to Pharaoh to bring my people the Israelites
out of Egypt." (Exodus 3:5-10)

Moses didn't know it, but Reluctance, a cousin of Rebellion, was
hanging out on that mountain too. God had chosen Moses—called him to
a life of service—and intended to involve him in his plan. But Reluctance
was right there, whispering in Moses' ear, prompting him to question God.

Why me?

Who are you?

What if your plan doesn't work?

What if I don't have it in me?

God had answers for each of Moses' questions. The most powerful
answer, though, was **"I AM."** Those two words answered all of Moses'
questions.

Why me? Because **I AM** God and I have a plan.

Who are you? **I AM WHO I AM**—your faithful God who always has
been and always will be.

What if your plan doesn't work? It will, because **I AM WHO I AM.** Need
physical proof? Throw down your staff. See what happens.

What if I don't have it in me? **I AM** the source of all strength. I will give
you what you need. Now go!

Moses went on to do the work God put in front of him. Reluctance
went with Moses, but God saw to it that his will was done anyway. God
accomplished great things and blessed many people through Moses. All
this happened when Moses finally listened to God's answers and went
to work.

When I began my 180 journey, I had lots of questions too. *Why love
God more? Can I love God more? How do I love God more (especially with
all my weaknesses and failures)?* I wanted answers to these questions. In
the same way that God conversed with Moses and answered all of his
questions, God used my 180 journey—the time I spent in the Word and
prayer—to answer mine.

"**I AM**" is the answer to all my questions. "I AM" is God's name and, as we learned in an earlier chapter, it represents the completeness of God. His holy, powerful, and unchanging nature. His worthiness.

During my 180 journey, it became clear that the purest and truest love for God is loving him for who **he is.** After all, that's how God sees me: Wearing Christ's righteousness, I am his own dear child. He loves me for who I am in Christ. His Old Testament covenant of love was fulfilled in Christ's life, death, and resurrection. And because of that, we have the New Testament corollary to "I AM": God *is* love.

All my questions can be answered by the essence of who God is.

Why love God more? Because **I AM WHO I AM**—your faithful God who always has been and always will be. I have promised and fulfilled my covenant of love with you. **I AM** love.

Can I love God more? **I AM** God and **I AM** love. You are able to love because I first loved you (1 John 4:19). Just do the work I put in front of you and see what happens.

How do I love God more? **I AM** love. **I AM** the power source (1 John 4:7). Put me first and watch how I bless you.

Indeed, God promises to bless those who love him—in multiple ways, as we'll explore in the last section of the book. I admit that blessings were a motivator for me to love God more. Who wouldn't want to take God up on his promises of protection (Psalm 91), wealth (Proverbs 8), grace (Ephesians 6), and more? Blessings are not the ultimate motivation, though. God is worthy of our praise simply because he is God. St. Bernard of Clairvaux noted that the promise of reward is an incredibly weak reason to love God: "It is the reluctant, not the eager, whom we urge by promises of reward.... One who loves God truly asks no other recompense than God Himself; for if he should demand anything else it would be the prize that he loved and not God" (Clairvaux, *On Loving God*).

And yet, how patiently and graciously God deals with his children. When I AM WHO I AM is too much for us to comprehend, his blessings are tools he uses to keep us close to him. He meets the reluctant with whatever blessing is needed to draw us closer: In the case of Moses, it was miraculous signs. For others of us, it might be a supportive friend or a touching song. God does not bribe, but he will do whatever it takes to draw us to him—to the foot of the cross where we can plainly see that he gave us himself, restored us to himself, and called us to a life of love.

Who of us can love God perfectly—simply for who he is? We can aspire to it, but as imperfect human beings we will always struggle with questions. For Moses, I AM WHO I AM could not be comprehended as reason enough to change careers and defy the world's most powerful leader. Moses was not yet spiritually mature enough for this amazing truth—I AM WHO I AM—to motivate him. Moses asked for more, and God gave Moses enough to strengthen him on his spiritual journey. None of us will be able to fully understand the complete meaning of I AM WHO I AM or "God is love" until we are in heaven with him.

In the meantime, here we are, called to love and serve God and others. Although blessings are not a reason to love God more, they sure are a nice benefit given to God's dearly loved children. It is God's will that we should have them. St. Bernard wrote, "Although God would be loved without respect to reward, yet he wills not to leave love unrewarded."

In the next section, we'll explore a few of the many blessings God promises to those who love him.

YOUR TURN:

- As a child of God, do you expect to be blessed? Why?
- Think of a time when you questioned whether God was working all things for good. Did that situation make you doubt his love for you or his loving plan for your life?
- How did God work through your doubt to bring you closer to him?

BENEFITS OF LOVING GOD MORE

We're Given Meaningful Work

"Do you love me?"

—Jesus

The boat rocked to and fro in the morning breeze. They'd been out on the lake all night and caught nothing. Peter's stomach churned like the dark water underneath his boat.

He was trying to make sense of the events of the last few weeks. He knew that Jesus had risen from the dead, just as he said he would. Peter had seen him twice in the last several days. But only briefly. Before those brief and unexpected encounters, Peter had denied Jesus in the courtyard while Jesus was on trial. Peter hadn't even had a chance to explain himself. Or apologize. Things had been so crazy lately.

Last night he couldn't sleep a wink. So he and his friends decided to make themselves useful—maybe catch some fish. Well, that wasn't working. Peter was restless. Maybe they ought to just row in and scrounge up some breakfast.

Just then, they heard a voice calling from the direction of the shoreline: "Friends, haven't you any fish?"

Peter was busy trying to set the oars in place so they could row in. "Nah," he called back over his shoulder, still agitated.

"Why don't you throw your net on the other side of the boat? You'll find fish there."

What did this guy know? Peter thought. *We've been out here all night.* But Thomas bought in hook, line, and sinker. He was already throwing the net over the opposite side of the boat. John wasn't helping Thomas at all. He was peering intently at the shoreline. The net began to fill with fish.

Then John elbowed Peter. "It is the Lord!"

What? Peter found new energy. "Let's row!" he cried.

Wait. The nets. Can't row with the nets down. So Peter grabbed his robe and jumped into the water. He made a beeline for the shore to see his friend, his Lord.

Once there, he found that Jesus had a campfire going, with fish and bread ready for breakfast. Peter's stomach stopped churning and instead started to growl.

"Hey! Peter!" Nathanael called from the boat. "Aren't you going to help us?"

Jesus smiled at Peter. "Better go get some of those fish you caught."

Peter obeyed and went to help his friends drag the net ashore. It was full of fish.

The story from John chapter 21 continues:

> When they had finished eating, Jesus said to Simon Peter, "Simon son of John, do you love me more than these?"
>
> "Yes, Lord," he said, "you know that I love you."
>
> Jesus said, "Feed my lambs."
>
> Again Jesus said, "Simon son of John, do you love me?"
>
> He answered, "Yes, Lord, you know that I love you."
>
> Jesus said, "Take care of my sheep."
>
> The third time he said to him, "Simon son of John, do you love me?"
>
> Peter was hurt because Jesus asked him the third time, "Do you love me?" He said, "Lord, you know all things; you know that I love you." (John 21:15–17)

About a week earlier, Peter had been sitting by another fire, outside of a courtroom, robe tucked in around him and hands warming. His friend

Jesus was not with him then, because Peter had deserted him. Jesus had been led away to a secret dead-of-night court trial, falsely accused, with all the corrupt powers of the Jewish state against him. But Peter had done worse than deserting Jesus. He shuddered to think of the events of that evening. He had done the unthinkable—something he had specifically and emphatically promised Jesus he would never do, even if it cost him his life. He publicly denied even knowing Jesus. Not once, but three times. And after he had done so, there was his Lord, bound and bloodied and sentenced to death and staring right at him as the guards led him by the courtyard and the rooster crowed.

And now Jesus was here, *three times* questioning Peter's love for him. Why? How could Peter explain how sorry he felt?

Jesus had the answer. *Here's how to show your feelings toward me:* "Feed my sheep" (John 21:17).

The account of Peter's reinstatement provides a model for those of us who want to understand what loving God means and how we are blessed by it. First, we see Peter, antsy and restless after the gut-wrenching events of his past several weeks, jumping with unbridled enthusiasm at the chance to see his Lord. He had tried to keep himself busy with fishing. He missed his friend, though, and he longed for the chance to reconcile. He knew that Jesus' forgiveness would calm his unsettled emotions.

Then, as he sits with Jesus by the fire, Jesus poses the question, "Do you love me more than these?" (Bear with me once again as I try to talk about the Greek words behind our English translation of these verses.) The word Jesus uses for "love" here is *agape*. Jesus wants to know if Peter loves him with all his heart, soul, and mind. Would Peter deny himself and lay down his life for Jesus out of sacrificial love?

Peter answers, "Yes, Lord. You know that I love you." Peter uses a different word for love than Jesus used: the word *philia*. The People's Bible analysis of this passage suggests that Peter is being humble (Gary Baumler, The People's Bible, *John*, p. 271). Peter knows Jesus can see into his heart. Peter knows that loving God with the *agape* kind of love is a tall order, especially for someone who so recently denied even knowing Jesus. So, in humility that is uncharacteristic of Peter and indicative of lessons learned, Peter answers that he thinks well of Jesus as his friend—*philia* love. My *Concordia Self-Study Bible* notes that the word *philia* in Peter's response refers to "spontaneous or natural affection or fondness in which emotion plays a more prominent role than will." It is as if Peter says, *Jesus, you know how very much I like you.*

Jesus gives Peter a task: "Feed my lambs."

Then he asks again, "Do you love me?" *Agape.*

Peter has to be wondering, *Did he not hear me?* But he doesn't ask. He again refers to Jesus' omniscience. "Yes, Lord, you know that I love you." *Philia.*

Once again, Jesus points to the work that needs to be done: "Take care of my sheep."

A third time, no doubt a parallel to Peter's threefold denial, Jesus asks, "Do you love me?" Jesus eases up and uses *philia* this time, as if to say, "Okay, Peter. You have shown me where your heart is."

Although Peter was hurt, it's important to note that Peter did not ask questions of his own in an effort to understand what his Lord was doing here. There was no Rebellion or Reluctance on the beach that morning— only the Lord and his dearly loved and forgiven disciple, sitting together, discussing the work that needed to be done.

Again Peter answered, "Lord, you know all things; you know that I love you."

In this account we see an incredibly emotional and impulsive servant of Christ who, having rebelled and repented, was now reinstated by Jesus. In the calming presence of Jesus, we see Peter answering his Savior's call with what he knows to be true. He abandons his propensity for over-the-top proclamations (John 13:37). Instead, he listens as Jesus gives him a special task—the care and feeding of other souls. It's a task that would require Peter to draw his strength from the deep reservoir of Jesus' love for him.

Meaningful work is a blessing given to those who love God. The repentant are renewed, reinstated, and then called to serve according to his purpose. Not everyone is called into a very public ministry like Peter was—in fact, relatively few are. But the Lord puts meaningful work in front of each of us. "There are different kinds of service, but the same Lord. There are different kinds of working, but in all of them and in everyone it is the same God at work" (1 Corinthians 12:5,6). I've found that to be true in my 180 experience as I have observed others around me. God created some people to be mandolin-playing dog trainers, some to be happy-dancing occupational therapists, some to be elders on church boards, and some to be cancer survivors. He has purposefully taken some of his children home to heaven early—like my husband's parents, Ted and Judy—and some he has allowed to live long, fruitful lives—like Grandma Molkentin, who you'll read about next. God is working through all of these people to bring his children closer to him and to put the story of his love on display.

YOUR TURN:

- If you were sitting on a beach with Jesus and he asked you if you love him, how would you respond?
- What tasks has Jesus set before you to give you opportunity to show Christian love?
- How does your life and work tell the story of God's love?

Rescued for a Reason

What if, on the playground all those years ago, I had heard, *"Red Rover, Red Rover, let Angie come over!"* and—instead of breaking into a run—what if I had sat down? My team would have been extremely frustrated with me. My name had been called, and it was my turn to run. The calling of my name was a call to action.

The same is true for Christians. God calls each of us by name when we hear the good news of what Jesus did to deliver us from our human predicament. That includes a call to action— living a Christian life, and loving and serving others.

My catechism has big words for God's work in the lives of Christians: First, there's **justification** (God's declaration that I am "not guilty" because Jesus paid for my sins), followed by **sanctification** (the process of the Holy Spirit helping me gladly turn away from sin and eagerly live a fruitful life). The first is what God did *for* me. The second is what he does *in* me, every day, especially as I remember my baptism.

There is purpose behind God's dealings with us, and it is more than deliverance. He rescued us to fulfill his purposes. "We are God's handiwork, created in Christ Jesus to do good works, which God prepared in advance for us to do" (Ephesians 2:10).

Grandma M.

"Walk in obedience to all that the LORD your God has commanded you, so that you may live and prosper and prolong your days in the land that you will possess."
—Deuteronomy 5:33

Grandma Molkentin has lived a full life. Born in 1920, she was the youngest of three children. Her parents spoke German as their first language and, as such, Grandma is fluent in both German and English. Education was extremely important to Grandma's family. Although everyone worked hard on the farm, Grandma and her siblings attended school and eventually college, which was rather unusual for a farming family at that time. Grandma lived through the Great Depression, and whenever I asked her about that time period, she always talked about God's providence. Their family farm was a place where extended family could come for food and work when needed.

Grandma taught elementary school for two years before meeting Grandpa, a young seminary student. They married and Grandma followed the young clergyman blissfully into the mission field, uncertain of the terrain ahead. Grandma's health challenges threatened her ability to have children and indeed took one child home to heaven as an infant. But her four living children have given her 13 grandchildren and 35 great grandchildren. She lived in parsonages in five states and served alongside Grandpa in multiple congregations. She never had a driver's license due to those lingering health problems. But that never bothered her too much, because she and Grandpa were always together, all the way up to the day Grandpa's death parted them in 2002.

I love it when Grandma reminisces, and when I visit, I listen eagerly. There is such a calm, quiet confidence in her demeanor. Her life is a model of quiet service, seeking God's will, and delighting in it.

"When I think of it all now, I just can't believe that this was my life," she said one day during one of our visits. It happened to be Day 96 of my 180, and I noticed the coincidence that Grandma was 96 years old at the time. Perhaps there would be something special about this particular visit.

Indeed, there was. During our visit, Grandma turned our conversation from looking backward on her life to looking at the present day, where she was in that moment. She told me all about the people and happenings in her retirement community. She loved living there for many reasons, one of which was the number of Christian friends who lived around her. The family had chosen this particular retirement community for Grandma for this very reason. She would have fellowship and connections with people she knew through Grandpa's lifelong service in the ministry. You've heard of "six degrees of separation"? In the Lutheran world, you can usually find a conversation-worthy connection with someone else who has served in the ministry. Grandma is masterful at finding those connections.

Recently, however, the retirement community had been sold to an investor group. It was no longer run by Christians and no longer designated as a distinctly Christian facility. The crosses that hung on the walls had come down, replaced with rather typical institutional décor. Where the three biggest crosses had hung in the lobby, honoring the greatest gift of all time, a clock now hung, cruelly marking time for these elderly residents. New people began moving in, many of whom Grandma did not know, no matter how hard she tried to make a connection. And many of the new residents were not Christian.

On this particular day, Grandma told me all about the disappearance of the Christian symbols and the loss of the familiar Christian affinity she had with the residents. She told me about a lady she saw quite frequently who never came to church services and did not pray with them at meals. All of this clearly bothered Grandma. Then she sighed and the edges of her mouth curved up into a smile. "Well," she said. "I guess God still has work for me to do."

My heart warmed at the thought of Grandma finding purpose in her daily life. I marveled at how God had brought disruption into this woman's peaceful life, yet she still is using her energy to serve him, to extend his love to those around her. One might say she has led a full life (past tense), but Grandma isn't done yet. Reluctance may whisper, "What can an old woman do?" But Grandma is still seeking God's will for her life. "Here I am," she responds to her Lord, with the strength he provides. God does not call us home until his work through us is finished.

God Calls Grandma Home

On December 1, 2017, while this book was in its editing phase, God called Grandma home to heaven. Her children, grandchildren, and great grandchildren celebrated her life at her Christian funeral. We all marveled at how God raised up this little farm girl to touch so many lives.

God used Grandma for his glory right up until her dying breath at age 97. The family received a beautiful note from one of the hospice nurses who cared for Grandma:

Thank you for your kind words and sharing your mom with me! I wanted to share with you the impact you and your mom have had on me. Until about a week ago, I was completing my master's degree as a family nurse practitioner. A week ago, while sitting on the floor next to your mom, I was thinking of her amazing life and her legacy and my moments with her struck me more than I can even understand. I went home and told my family that I was no longer becoming an FNP but a geriatric nurse practitioner and ultimately a hospice nurse practitioner. When asked why the change, I was able to say that God sent me an angel to help me write my legacy. So just as you've told me that I was sent to help on this journey, she was also sent to me and I'm so blessed to have gotten a little time with her.

We are all blessed to be in the company of those whose lives are evidence of God's love story. My 180 journey has opened my eyes to see people who love God in their own unique ways, wherever God has placed them. I appreciate them more. The emotion I felt at Grandma's funeral was that of intense gratitude that God had given me and others such a wonderful example of Christian living in Grandma M.

We Have Guidance

"I will not leave you as orphans; I will come to you."

—John 14:18

On the day in 1942 when Grandma and Grandpa Molkentin got into a car to make their long drive to the mission fields of Arizona, they had little knowledge of the road before them. They were newlyweds, navigating the ins and outs of a fresh marriage and excited to begin their journey together. They set out with no GPS, no internet to check the weather ahead, no AAA roadside insurance in case something went wrong. There was no such thing as "text me when you get there" to reassure their loved ones who were waving goodbye. All they had was a map, a letter from the mission board, gas ration coupons, and whatever belongings fit into their car. And, of course, they took with them the promises from God's Word that he would be with them, watch over them, and guide them in their mission work.

I, of course, did not know Grandma back then, but I do know from our conversations that being in God's Word was a lifelong habit for Grandma. God's Word was present in her home as a child. God's Word went with her and Grandpa to Arizona and throughout their travels. Even when Grandma's main mode of transportation was her wheelchair, she never rolled out the door without her devotion book. Ask anyone who visited her—God's Word was her guide.

I've mentioned frequently that my 180 journey was a rediscovery of the importance of God's Word in my daily life. The Holy Spirit used the Word to soften my heart and bring back some of the joy of my salvation. I was reminded that God not only rescued me but that he has meaningful plans for me. Why had that been so hard to grasp at the beginning of my 180 journey? I bemoan my feeble brain and my human weakness! God's communication in his Word has been right there from the beginning. I had forgotten about the blessing of his guidance. My head knowledge had told me that the chief purpose of God's Word is to reveal the story of God's love for us and how his plan for our salvation unfolded. "These are the very Scriptures that testify about me," Jesus says in John 5:39. But its value doesn't end there. God's Word also serves as a guide for our lives:

"Your word is a lamp for my feet, a light on my path" (Psalm 119:105). God blesses those who love him with his constant guidance and communication in the form of his Word.

To understand how God intends to bless those who love him, let's go back to the story of the people of Israel. As you know by now, I am particularly fascinated by the people of Israel because I have learned so much from watching how God provided for them and disciplined them. I see myself in their behavior: the same off-and-on rebellion, forgetfulness, and ingratitude. And so, God's words to his people of Israel are very relevant to me today, particularly those in Deuteronomy, the first place God recorded the command to love him with all of our hearts, souls, and minds. When God gave this original command, he certainly knew his children would continue to struggle to love him. He anticipated it and provided some extremely important guidance that would help them keep such an important command. Here is God's guidance from Deuteronomy chapters 6 and 7, still relevant to you and me today:

Keep the commands in front of you. "These commandments that I give you today are to be on your hearts. Impress them on your children. Talk about them when you sit at home and when you walk along the road, when you lie down and when you get up. Tie them as symbols on your hands and bind them on your foreheads. Write them on the doorframes of your houses and on your gates" (Deuteronomy 6:6-9). God was warning his people against the absence-makes-the-heart-grow-fonder mentality. A loving relationship with God means literally weaving his words and symbols into our lives—spiritually and physically (see sidebar "Practical Pillars").

Notice that I am providing for you. "When the LORD your God brings you into the land he swore to your fathers, to Abraham, Isaac and Jacob, to give you—a land with large, flourishing cities you did not build, houses filled with all kinds of good things you did not provide, wells you did not dig, and vineyards and olive groves you did not plant—then when you eat and are satisfied, be careful that you do not forget the LORD, who brought you out of Egypt, out of the land of slavery" (Deuteronomy 6:10-12). Here God was reminding his children that he has kept his promises to preserve and provide for them. This prompts me to think about how God has done the same for me and my family. It prompts me to ask, *Am I grateful?*

Tell the story. "In the future, when your son asks you, 'What is the meaning of the stipulations, decrees and laws the LORD our God has commanded you?' tell him: 'We were slaves of Pharaoh in Egypt, but the LORD brought us out of Egypt with a mighty hand. Before our eyes the LORD sent signs and wonders—great and terrible—on Egypt and Pharaoh and his whole household. But he brought us out from there to bring us in and give us the land he promised on oath to our ancestors. The LORD commanded us to obey all these decrees and to fear the LORD our God, so that we might always prosper and be kept alive, as is the case today'" (Deuteronomy 6:20-24). Here God reminds us about more of the "why" behind our rescue—to have a nation of people who love him and as a result guard and keep his commands. Further, God's people will tell the next generation the story of God's love: We fallen human beings were destined to a life of slavery, not to cruel pharaohs and Egyptians, but to sin and sin's power. But he rescued us from that destiny. And he did so in an amazing and wonderful way, with "signs and wonders"—the virgin birth of his Son, taking on flesh and doing for us what we were powerless to do. When my children ask questions like, "Why do we set aside Sunday for church?" or "Why is it so important to you that I choose a spouse who loves God?" I need to be prepared to tell the story of our rescue—he brought us out of our predicament and into a life that glorifies him.

Remember, love is the reason. "The LORD did not set his affection on you and choose you because you were more numerous than other peoples, for you were the fewest of all peoples. But it was because the LORD loved you and kept the oath he swore to your ancestors that he brought you out with a mighty hand and redeemed you from the land of slavery, from the power of Pharaoh king of Egypt. Know therefore that the LORD your God is God; he is the faithful God, keeping his covenant of love to a thousand generations of those who love him and keep his commandments" (Deuteronomy 7:7-9). Nothing that we did (or that we were going to do for him) caused God to intervene on our behalf as he did. He did it because he loves us and is faithful. Love is the reason behind the rescue, and love is the reason he desires an ongoing, special relationship with us.

Do not be afraid. "You may say to yourselves, 'These nations are stronger than we are. How can we drive them out?' But do not be afraid of them; remember well what the LORD your God did to Pharaoh and to all Egypt. You saw with your own eyes the great trials, the signs and wonders, the mighty hand and outstretched arm, with which the LORD your God brought you out. The LORD your God will do the same to all the peoples you now fear. Do not be terrified by them, for the LORD your God, who is among you, is a great and awesome God. The LORD your God will drive out those nations before you, little by little. You will not be allowed to eliminate them all at once, or the wild animals will multiply around you. But the LORD your God will deliver them over to you" (Deuteronomy 7:17-19,21-23). When the people of Israel arrived in the Promised Land, it wasn't empty. Other nations of people had settled there and were standing in the way of God's plan unfolding. It can be very troubling to think about all the battles, death, and destruction that occurred in order for the people of Israel to repossess the Promised Land. In fact, it might be difficult to think about how a loving God could direct (or even command) all of this combat. Yet, if God's plan for salvation had not unfolded, all human beings would face eternal destruction. And so, God helped the people of Israel win their battles, one by one, until his purposes were achieved.

This passage does not only apply to the people of Israel when they were faced with enemies on their journey; its encouragement, "Do not be terrified," also speaks to all Christians of all time, including a busy mother who feels overwhelmed by all the challenges of life. Or the tender-hearted Christian who sees all the people in need and feels overwhelmed by the task. Or the 96-year-old who is praying for strength to do the work set before her. God's everlasting love for his children includes the promise that there is eventual victory for those who love him. Maybe not "all at once." Most likely not all at once. That can be tough to remember, and God knew it. That's why he issued the reminder.

The more I study the people of Israel, the more I see myself in their story. God brought the people of Israel out of slavery, and they complained that they would be better off where they had been (Exodus 17:3). *That's me when I rebel against God's love for me and the salvation he provided.* He chose them as his special people, and they did not want to be unique or special or set apart (1 Samuel 8). *That's me when I rebel against being chosen.* The Old Testament narratives of the people of Israel illustrate how quickly and easily we human beings turn against God, how our rebellion grieves God, how he continues to love steadfastly, and how his plan is in motion for our ultimate good. Psalm 78 sums up God's patience toward the ingratitude of the people of Israel (and mine too) quite well: "Yet [God] was merciful; he forgave their iniquities and did not destroy them. Time after time he restrained his anger and did not stir up his full wrath. He remembered that they were but flesh" (Psalm 78:38,39).

He remembers that I am but flesh. He knows I need guidance.

In the Old Testament, God's guidance often took on visible or audible form: A pillar of cloud. A pillar of fire. A smoke-covered mountain.

A clear voice heard by his chosen leaders. Today he guides us through the Word and the Holy Spirit working through that Word, "that we may understand what God had freely given us" (1 Corinthians 2:12). Before leaving his disciples, Jesus explained that we are not left as orphans—that it would be the Holy Spirit's job to guide us "into all the truth" (John 16:13). Ongoing guidance in the form of the Word and Spirit are blessings for those who love God.

YOUR TURN:

- What conditions cause you to doubt that God is really with you?
- How does God's specific guidance for the people of Israel help you keep doubts at bay?
- Read Psalm 78 in its entirety. Do you see yourself in the description of the people of Israel? What does the Psalm say about our responsibility to the next generation of children?
- What "practical pillars" can you use in your life as visual reminders of God's guidance?

Practical Pillars

As they set out on their journey from Egypt, God gave the people of Israel his own special GPS: "By day the LORD went ahead of them in a pillar of cloud to guide them on their way and by night in a pillar of fire to give them light, so that they could travel by day or night" (Exodus 13:21).

When the people of Israel reached the border of the Promised Land, God no longer used this very visible form of guidance. Instead, through Moses' speech beginning in Deuteronomy chapter 6, God gives his children practical advice for keeping him visible and relevant in their daily lives. We can apply this advice in our lives today:

○ **Memorization:** God says to keep his commands "on your hearts." Committing passages to memory keeps them with us and helps us recall them when needed.

○ **Regular meditation:** God says to talk about his commands "when you lie down and when you get up," suggesting a regular pattern of meditating at key points during our day.

○ **Conversations as we "walk along the road":** Although modern life has us taking planes, trains, and automobiles, the concept is still the same. Our vehicles can be great places for conversations seasoned with God's Word. I've found that to be true with my children: When they were young, we played Christian music in the car. Now that they are teenagers, we have some of our best conversations driving to and from activities. And that chatty person next to you on the airplane? God may be giving you an opportunity to share his Word. (Hint: Regular meditation and memorization prepares us for these conversations.)

○ **Wearables:** When God talks about tying his commands "as symbols on your hands" or foreheads, he's not dictating what we should wear; rather, he's encouraging us to put his words in places where we (and sometimes other people too) can see them. Wearing Christian jewelry, hats, and t-shirts reminds us of who God is and who we are.

○ **Home decor:** God encourages his children to put his words in prominent places, such as "on the doorframes of your houses and on your gates." Once again, God is not *commanding* us to use Christian decor. He is encouraging us to put his words in places where we will be daily reminded of him as we come and go. Our decor does not need to be expensive: some of my most treasured Christian decorations are craft projects made by my children.

The fact that God gave this practical guidance shows us how much God understands the challenges we face in trying to remember him and put him first in our lives. The world is big and noisy, and our journey (God willing) is long. God is with us through his Word and the Holy Spirit working within us—he promises that (Isaiah 59:21). He also encourages us to use "practical pillars" as physical reminders of his Word and his promises.

We Have a Promise

"If we find ourselves with a desire that nothing in this world can satisfy, the most probable explanation is that we were made for another world."

—C. S. Lewis

I remember a Sunday morning worship service a long time ago that was particularly moving. (It must have been incredible for me to remember it after all this time!) I remember sitting in a big, full church building, singing the hymn "For All the Saints" with hundreds of other voices. There was an organ and tympani and trumpets. The words of the hymn combined with the majestic music and all those voices singing together made my spine tingle.

> And when the fight is fierce, the warfare long,
> Steals on the ear the distant triumph song,
> And hearts are brave again and arms are strong.
> Alleluia! Alleluia! (*Christian Worship* 551:5)

I remember thinking, *This must be what heaven feels like.* A chorus of Christians singing together. Victory is at hand. No worry, no stress, no physical ailments, no insecurities. Just joyful celebration of victory.

That moment was a marriage of head knowledge and Spirit-led emotion. The result was euphoric. God in his wisdom allowed me to have that emotional experience, to give me a taste of the joy that awaits in heaven. What a blessing to have those moments! Emotional highs are a gift, while the valleys serve to remind us that we're not in heaven yet. While we wait for that glorious day, we're figuring out how to love and serve God with whatever blessings he's given us. Hopefully the story of my 180 journey has provided you with some valuable suggestions for loving God and others as you await the joys of heaven.

We can't even imagine the joy God has in store for his children, both for this life, as we follow him faithfully, and in heaven. We children of God have been given an incredible promise:

> "What no eye has seen,
> what no ear has heard,
> and what no human mind has conceived"—

the things God has prepared for those who love him—
these are the things God has revealed to us by his Spirit.
(1 Corinthians 2:9,10)

Someday I will hear the trumpet call, and I will be caught up together with my fellow believers in the clouds (1 Thessalonians 4:17) to be with Jesus forever. I will have a perfectly transformed heart, mind, and body in heaven. All my questions will be answered. Rebellion will cease. Reluctance will melt away. I will experience perfect love in my own flesh—body, mind, spirit together. "I, and not another," Job said with the confidence that had eluded him during the early days of his physical and spiritual struggle. "How my heart yearns within me!" (Job 19:27).

Until heaven, I can only imagine what perfect love is like. Until then, I wait—and live—as a child of the promise (Romans 9:8).

YOUR TURN:

- Have you ever had a moment where you said, "This must be what heaven feels like"?

- Imagine hearing the trumpet call and being absolutely confident that God is taking you home to heaven. What will you feel in that moment? Who will you want with you in that moment?

- How can you use your life now to help ensure that more of those you know and love are with you in heaven?

- What can you do to increase your joy now while you wait for the joys of heaven?

Jesus

"This is love: not that we loved God, but that he loved us and sent his Son as an atoning sacrifice for our sins."
—1 John 4:10

During my 180 journey, I became reacquainted with someone who has known me from the beginning. In fact, he knit me together in my mother's womb.

On the day of my baptism, his voice echoed through the church and indeed through all eternity, "Let Angie come over." That was the beginning of a run across the expanse of time.

I read his words often—sometimes because I want to and sometimes because duty calls. He has a way with words. He says things like, "I have loved you with an everlasting love" (Jeremiah 31:3) and "Though the mountains be shaken and the hills be removed, yet my unfailing love for you will not be shaken" (Isaiah 54:10). I've come to understand that he has a way with words because he *is* God's Word (John 1:1).

Many of the people I know also know him. I can see his influence in their lives. He is the steadiness in Sarah's demeanor. He is the reason Mr. Haferman's lips curl into a smile as he greets his students. He is the melody of Roger and Lela's beautiful music that touched the hearts of Bill and Susan. He is the strong silence that lives in my dad. He shines like the morning sun through Nan and keeps her cancer at bay. He is the rhythm of Dawn's happy dance and the reason she exudes love in everything she does. He manages the time on the clock at Grandma's retirement home, and he gave her the grace and strength to be his witness even when the symbols of his presence were removed. And he is part of my family. Whenever my children talk about him, I'm reminded of how wonderful it is to be chosen, how wonderful it is that we are all connected for eternity through him, as his children with the promise of heaven.

He is well acquainted with Rebellion too. He is the role model for me in conversations with her, always with a word to put her in her place. But he went even further on my behalf. He confronted the reason behind Rebellion—*sin.* He went right to the root of the human predicament, to the cross, where he gave himself up as the final sacrifice for sin. His words, "It is finished," were the final admonition for Rebellion. Yes, his life was an example for me, but he didn't come here just to show me how to be a little more loving. In fact, the more kindness he showed during his life and the more miracles he did, the more people hated him, revealing just how incurable the human condition is. He, God's Son, became more than an example—he became the atoning sacrifice for me, for all people. Yes, Rebellion had her time with me, and she is still running interference as I try to love God more and love others the way Jesus did. *But she won't win in the end* because of his sacrificial love for me.

When people speak of love—or try to describe it—they struggle to find the words. They write songs and poetry and movies that try to define it. What God has done is the essence of love. I don't think I'll ever fully grasp how great God's love is for me. That it just *is*—and how big that is. But I am thankful that I know him. I am thankful for all the pictures and stories and people who point me to him and encourage me to remain in him. The objective truth of what Jesus did *for me* has the power to stir emotion *in me*.

This is love.

My Next Turn

"I press on toward the goal to win the prize for which God has called me heavenward in Christ Jesus."

—Philippians 3:14

I began my 180 with a less than thankful heart. I was doubtful that loving God more had any purpose. After all, he is who he is. *Would it matter if I loved him more? And what would loving God more look like? Feel like?*

So many deep questions! With my relationship on autopilot, I had not taken the time to explore any of them. It took my 180 journey to move my relationship with God off of autopilot. Spending intentional time together in the Word and in prayer helped rekindle the relationship and allowed the Holy Spirit to fan the flame of faith.

That's what a 180 journey really is—time. It was not about a dramatic change in my behavior (although the changes God worked in me were pretty amazing). Rather, it was about our time spent together—God and me. That intentional time strengthened the relationship. God reminded me of who he is and what he has done for me. He also helped me better understand who I am in him. In that sense, maybe the Beatles were on to something when they wrote this line into their 1967 anthem about love: "Nothing you can do, but you can learn how to be you in time." My 180 was about what God did for me and in me over time. In the process, I learned how to be thankful and joyful for who I am in Christ. My journey toward loving God more helped me learn how to be me in time.

All the learnings I've described in this book have been enriching and wonderful. And I know I still have a long way to go when it comes to loving God more. There are many others who exhibit love for God much more boldly than I do: Those who go into dangerous parts of the world as missionaries. Those who give extraordinary amounts of time or money to bring food and medical care through Christian love and service. Those who hold up John 3:16 signs in public settings, despite scoffs and ridicule. Those who praise God's name in the face of challenging health issues or disabilities. I deserve no accolades for making it through 180 days of reading God's Word at the comfort of my kitchen table. Somewhere in the world, Christians are risking their lives to huddle around a Bible to be strengthened for their fight against Rebellion *and* worldly authorities who would have them killed. The world needs more of these people. The world needs more people with courage and zeal and demonstrable devotion to God without excuses or rationalization. If I want to be this kind of person, I know I'll have to turn up the level of discipline in my life. Perhaps I'll try a 180 on another topic: trusting God more, praying to God more, or witnessing more. I certainly do not want to slide backward into a life that takes for granted all God has done for me. "So, if you think you are standing firm, be careful that you don't fall!" (1 Corinthians 10:12). *Remember what I have done for you. Remember who you are.*

My 180 journey was a great way to rediscover and remember important truths. I am excited to try another one and see what happens.

TRAVEL TIPS:

○ There are more books in the My 180 series, each written by a different author who focuses on a different aspect of a Christian's relationship with God. The series has been planned to include topics such as "Waiting On God More," "Trusting God More," "Thanking God More," and "Fearing God More."

○ At the time of this writing, I had not yet read any of the other books in this series. I simply mention them to you now because knowing they are available may help you determine the best topic for a 180 journey of your own.

○ All the books in the My 180 series will be available at nph.net.

Ready for Your Turn?

"Examine yourselves to see whether you are in the faith."

—2 Corinthians 13:5

Are you ready to try a 180 of your own? Hopefully the story of my journey has intrigued you. Your journey will be different from mine, because you are your own person with your own personal strengths, weaknesses, experiences, and social circles. You may want to study a different topic, such as trusting God more or praising God more. No matter how you decide to construct your 180, I'll encourage you with one final piece of advice: *Keep it simple.*

Why? That's what God wants for us. That's what Sarah kept reminding me to do whenever I got all balled up trying to understand the big topic of love.

As deep and astounding as God's love is for us, he himself desires a simple, loving relationship with us. You'll recall from the opening chapters of this book that we heard a description of this simplicity from the prophet Jeremiah. As God called Israel back from rebellion, he described a simpler time when he and his people enjoyed a close relationship, much as newlyweds enjoy the honeymoon period of their marriage (Jeremiah 2:2). There is an analogy here for our Christian walk today. For those of us who have been lifelong Christians, think about this: Before we really began our journey on the road of life, before all the crazy busyness and challenges of making a living and making sense of it all, there was a beautiful, simple relationship that for many of us began at our baptism. In the early years of our Christian walk, perhaps as children, we followed him, singing "Jesus loves me" and "I am trusting you, Lord Jesus." We put God first. Then what happened? Maybe we began to accumulate things, responsibilities, and blessings that threatened the simple relationship (as Jesus described in Luke chapter 8, the parable of the sower). If you are new to Christianity, the danger of a lukewarm relationship exists for you as well. In any relationship, it is easy to take each other for granted. To get bored. To become distracted. Except in our relationship with God, he does not move; his love is steadfast and everlasting. It is we, his children, who are constantly at risk of turning away and forsaking his love.

That's why God reminds us over and over again to "remain in" him. There is nothing fancy or complicated about that word—*remain*. The apostle John repeats this thought multiple times in his gospel and letters. The People's Bible on 1 John notes that the Greek word for "remain" is repeated 24 times in 1 John alone: "Why? Because it is human nature to drift. Because the sin within us causes people to give up, lose interest, grow bored, itch for novelty, be driven by their appetites instead of their heads" (Mark Jeske, The People's Bible, *James, 1,2 Peter, 1,2,3 John, Jude,* p. 231).

This refrain is worth repeating: The value of a 180 journey is being in God's Word in a focused and disciplined way over a period of time. This is where we meet Jesus. This is where Rebellion meets her match, Reluctance melts away, Repentance is stirred, and renewal happens in our hearts. This is where we're reminded of what love really is. This is where the Spirit is at work to guide us and to produce real, beautiful, abundant fruits of faith.

Are you ready for your turn? Try it! Trust the process. *See what happens.*

Here's my prayer for you—the words the apostle Paul prayed for Christians living at his time and throughout the ages to come:

> I pray that out of his glorious riches he may strengthen you with power through his Spirit in your inner being, so that Christ may dwell in your hearts through faith. And I pray that you, being rooted and established in love, may have power, together with all the Lord's holy people, to grasp how wide and long and high and deep is the love of Christ, and to know this love that surpasses knowledge—that you may be filled to the measure of all the fullness of God.
>
> Now to him who is able to do immeasurably more than all we ask or imagine, according to his power that is at work within us, to him be glory in the church and in Christ Jesus throughout all generations, for ever and ever! Amen. (Ephesians 3:16-21)

Feelings come and feelings go,
And feelings are deceiving;
My warrant is the Word of God—
Naught else is worth believing.

Though all my heart should feel condemned
For want of some sweet token,
There is One greater than my heart
Whose Word cannot be broken.

I'll trust in God's unchanging Word
Till soul and body sever,
For, though all things shall pass away,
His Word shall stand forever!

—anonymous poem based on words of Martin Luther

Appendix

My 180 Study Process:

- Pray daily for . . .
    - help to love God more
    - help to understand better what it means to love God more
    - help to notice other people who are good examples of loving God more
- Study weekly the Bible's teachings about loving God more
- Talk regularly with an accountability partner who agreed to go on the same journey
- Journal daily about learnings and experiences

Resources for Readings:

- *Concordia Self-Study Bible*—use for daily Bible readings, making use of the footnotes and cross references
- The People's Bible series (Bible commentaries)—use to illuminate passages where greater understanding is desired
- Luther's Small Catechism—use as a general study aid when questions arise

Sample Study Guide:

WEEKS 1 & 2: The command to love God—Deuteronomy 6:5; Matthew 22:37-39; Mark 12:30,31

WEEK 3: The source of all love—1 John 4:7-21; John 3:16; Ephesians 3:14-19; Deuteronomy 7:7-9

WEEK 4: God loved us first—Romans 5:1-11; Deuteronomy 7:6-24; Ephesians 2:4-7; Jeremiah 31; Romans 8:38,39

WEEK 5: To love God is to love others—John 15:1-17; John 13:34,35; 1 John 3:16

WEEKS 6 & 7: What loving God is—*On Loving God* by St. Bernard of Clairvaux

WEEK 8: What loving God looks like: gratefulness—Luke 7:36-50; Psalm 51:10-17; Psalm 103

WEEK 9: What loving God looks like: obedience—John 14:15-24; 1 John 5:1-6; John 15:9-19; Deuteronomy 6

WEEK 10: What loving God looks like: sight unseen—John 14:28-31; 1 Peter 1:3-9; 1 John 4:12

WEEK 11: What loving God looks like: reverent—Exodus 20:1-21; Malachi 1; Daniel 9:1-19; Psalm 95; Job 38

WEEK 12: Not enough to be "acquainted" with God—Revelation 2:1-6; 1 Corinthians 12:31–13:13; Jeremiah 2:1-3; Luke 13:22-30; Revelation 3:14-22

WEEK 13: Flex week—**Opportunity to . . .** reread favorite passages, pick previous passages that need more in-depth study, add readings that recently came to attention

WEEK 14: Love without reward—Luke 6:27-35; Psalm 51:15-17; Matthew 5:43-48

WEEK 15: Blessings promised to those who love God—Ephesians 6:24; 1 Corinthians 2:6-10; Proverbs 8:12-21; Deuteronomy 11:13-15

WEEK 16: Blessings promised to those who love God (continued)— Psalm 119:97-132; James 1:12; Psalm 91:14; Psalm 145:20; Psalm 37:4

WEEK 17: Love as the supreme virtue—Ephesians 3:16-19; 1 Corinthians 13; Colossians 3:12-14

WEEKS 18 & 19: Loving God is not a work that saves us—Apology to the Augsburg Confession, Article III: Of Love and Fulfilling the Law

WEEK 20: What Martin Luther said about love—*What Luther Says,* Volume 2: Love, Divine

WEEK 21: What Martin Luther said about love—*What Luther Says,* Volume 2: Love, Human

WEEK 22: Christ's model of love and service—John 13:1-17; Philippians 2:1-8

WEEK 23: The call to love and serve others—1 Peter 4:8-11; John 21:15-17

WEEK 24: My identity as a loved child of God—1 John 3:1-18

WEEK 25: Flex week—**Opportunity to . . .** reread favorite passages, pick previous passages that need more in-depth study, add readings that recently came to attention

FINAL DAYS: Review the journey—**Opportunity to . . .** look back on pages in journal, note areas of growth, note areas for continued growth, reflect on favorite experiences or passages